SOMEONE PUT A ROAD ON OUR CAVE

by Joe Graham

An autobiographical, tongue-in-cheek,

memoir of growing up on the

outskirts of Glasgow in the sixties.

For Jim and Wullie

Once a Daredevil...always a Daredevil.

EASTERHOUSE

NORTH TO
MILTON +
HIGHLANDS

TO
SCHOOL
+ CHAPEL

ENTER
AT
YOUR
PERIL

OUR
CLOSE

WULLIE'S
CLOSE

SWINGS

STAIRS

TURN
BACK

BULL
COW

FARMERS FIELD

DO
NOT
ENTER

3 AND IN
PITCH

WEE
HUMPS

5/11 PITCH

10/21 PITCH

PAUL'S
ROWE

MY
THE LONGY

THE
DEN

THE NOLLY

COALIE

TRAIN
STATION

NO
MAN'S
LAND

THE
TREE

REST
OF
WORLD

Contents

CHAPTER 1

A very good place to start

In the swinging sixties the world was on the eve of destruction, but we weren't really bothered, we had our own problems.

There wasn't a lot of swinging going on that we saw either. We had swings. We swung from things on occasion, but not enough for us to specifically label it 'The Swinging Sixties'. I spent more time on the roundabouts if I'm honest. They were safer. Some of them. Swings scared the life out of me.

One swing in particular 'The Swing', scared me the most. 'The Swing' was the scariest of all swings. If I had known then that I would eventually have to face 'The Swing', maybe I would have tried harder to conquer my fear of ordinary swings. But I didn't know 'The Swing' was coming. None of us did. Not me. Not Jim. Not Wullie. Not yet.

For now we were just three 'innocent' boys hanging around the swing park near the shops, pretending we didn't like swings. Pretending swings were for girls, who it seems had no fear of swings and would stand up on them; wrap legs around the chains; stand up two at a time, facing opposite directions; swing almost horizontal as if God meant for them to defy gravity. While three innocent boys, pretending we didn't like swings, looked on in awe and tried, in vain, to see up their skirts. Oh come on, they're upside down. What were we supposed to do? It's not as if we even knew what we were looking at or why we were looking, but we had to look. They are girls; we are boys; they have skirts; we have eyes. I didn't do the wiring, I'm just driving this thing.

I don't know why they had to call them swing parks. Adventure playground would have been a bit of a stretch to describe some swings, a roundabout and suspiciously sticky slide, so they had to call them something. Swings grabbed the moniker, which put pressure on you to take a turn on them in a playful yet sadistic version of circuit training. You try to make the slide as dangerous looking as you can, so that you can pretend you are too busy doing something macho to bother with girly swings. Some slides were actually pretty high and on those occasions you might have to invent a bad leg or risk dying of vertigo, if you can die of that. It's a wonder I got out of bed most days as it already looks like I was afraid of my own shadow. The swings had to be faced at some point. You can't stay on the sticky slide forever, unless you are actually stuck on there for real.

The biggest problem with swings is that from the ages of seven to twelve, you aren't allowed to sit casually on a normal swing and have a bit of a gentle sway. Not if you are a boy with other mates around. It was against all the boy rules back then.

You're allowed now. Oh, it's great now! No problem. Now that there are actual consequences of falling off a swing. For some reason no one over fifty can resist a swing. Makes them feel young and takes them back and oh, how we love to be taken back (says he writing a whole book on it). Does it really take them back or are they all just as scared as I was and trying to make it look like they always had the courage?

'Go on, have a bit of a sway.'

'Oh look at him having a bit of a sway.'

'I love a swing.'

'He loves a swing.'

Does he? Does he really?

'Takes me back.'

Does it? Does it really?

There's no stopping the old boy. Even happy to build up a bit of horizontal action.

'That's too much. Mind your hip. Mind your knees. Mind your back. Mind your piles. That's high enough. Off now! You'll break a hip. Off!! You proved you've still got it. Off!!'

I never had it.

If you so much as sat on a swing, you were expected to display the acrobatic skills, courage and daring of a Cirque de Soloeil clown. You were expected to go as high as possible. In fact you were expected to go right over the top, just to prove you could defy death more than the next terrified kid waiting his turn with crossed fingers and legs. And if you weren't going to do it yourself, someone was going to do it for you. Someone was going to push you until you wet yourself, fell off, cried for your mammy...or actually did it! I usually went for a combination of the first three options. Now all this was before we had any of those park rides that could turn you upside down, inside out and back to front. All that was really possible then was a bit of up and down roller coastering, which by today's standards was a ride in the tea cups.

Bear in mind that a disturbed child from the sixties, who was taunted and teased on the swings, was no doubt the engineering, criminal mastermind behind modern, disturbing theme park rides. Who else would come up with those things?

'Zey want to go right over, upsidey downy? Fine, I vill make zem go right over and over upsidey downy, till zey poopy zer pants, like I did. Zey vill vish zey never pushed me on ze swing. Ha ha ha ha ha ha...ha.'

Or it might have just been a girl.

Some roundabouts, to be fair, weren't any less terrifying. The nice cosy ones with wooden floors were great, but we didn't have one of those. Why have that when you can have some scaffolding poles welded into a rough octagonal shape and painted different colours to make it look fun. Fun? Fun was hanging on for grim death as the sadistic swing pushers moved to roundabout pushing whilst a dizzying mix of gravel and broken glass blurred past below you faster than that spinny astronaut thing, threatening to rip the skin off any boy who couldn't hold on. We didn't have any of that namby pamby rubber ground stuff they have now. My hands don't grip all the way around a scaffolding pole now, never mind then. If you felt yourself slipping, it was best not to let on. Better to hope they get bored before you slip off into the vortex they have created.

'I'm losing ma grip! I'm losing ma grip!'

'He's losing his grip!'

'Great, faster!!'

If you were coming off, so was half your skin, so you had to hang on. As if that isn't enough jeopardy, there are actually two ways to spin a roundabout which could potentially add to the horror. There is the normal way, and there is the 'sick' way. On a roundabout anti-clockwise is the sick way. If some sadistic spinner saw you were looking a bit scared, he would up the ante. Just as you think the damn thing is slowing and the ordeal is over, you realise he is just changing direction with a gleeful cry.

'Sick way!!'

I usually felt sick either way. I now realise two things about roundabouts; firstly, even fighter pilots get a little queasy at Mach 5, so it's no disgrace to feel sick. I do wonder if they test astronauts the normal way and the sick way; and secondly that, with enough incentive, two ten year old Glasgow boys can spin a roundabout faster than NASA. So even the very mention of swinging in the sixties sends me into a cold sweat.

It wasn't even the sixties anyway. I know the dates work out, but they don't mean anything. We only used calendars to keep track of Lent, not to check whether mini skirts were in that month. Every image of some hip, trendy, model or swinger striding down Carnaby Street in a vision of how everyone was so fashion conscious and aware of sexual liberation, is barking up the wrong loon pants of the world as we knew it. We were young, so fashion passed us by. Still passes me by, but that isn't the point. There was another sixties going on. The real one, that was actually a lot more like the fifties. I know we were children and in those days parents didn't make any attempt to dress their children in Baby Gap, so I'm not suggesting that we would have been aware of fashion trends anyway. What I am suggesting is our parents were no more aware of fashion trends than we were. They were still in the fifties and listening to Frank Sinatra from the forties. You never know what era you are in until after you've been in it. We didn't even know it was the sixties. We only know it was the sixties now. We just had no idea it was 'The Sixties' then.

So we are not venturing into the sixties here. We are venturing into a land and a time that we may as well have stumbled across through an old wardrobe. Why we were in an old wardrobe I have no idea. Perhaps looking for mum's Littlewoods catalogue to see the underwear section. Who knows? That was the normal reason to rummage in wardrobes. What were those Narnia kids looking for anyway?

What happened in the land we lived in is different from anything that went on beyond it. It was a closed world that only three of us were fully privy to. Others were allowed glimpses but only three of us saw it all. There were lots of extended family around at times; cousins, uncles and aunties, but they did not live fully in our world and I don't have enough information on them to write a pamphlet never mind a book.

I do a lot of nodding and smiling if anyone mentions names from the past, or even in our own family, that I should know. I'm assuming that if you don't move away from an area it is easier to recall names and faces as the triggers are still there and you even run into them on occasion. I moved south some years ago to find fame and fortune and I can see how that re-programmes your memory bank. But if I want to write about my childhood, I will have to break into that bank and see how much is still in there. How much of it still colours how I think and feel.

At lot of the names and places don't come flowing out of me as they do with some people. My siblings have a memory of characters and situations from my past that is encyclopedic in detail and even fully up to speed with their current situations. I generally have no idea who they are even talking about.

'You remember that auntie Brenda's oldest Robbie had twins with that woman from Coatbridge, Alexis, you remember?...'

I nod and smile. There was no pause for breath or punctuation.

'Yes of course you do anyway he left her after he caught her with that scabby looking bloke who worked in the City Bakeries and now it turns out that uncle Jimmy's second eldest boy Raymond, who also works at City Bakeries well he used to until he was suspended for eating the jelly gums off the top of the Eiffel Towers anyway he met her the other day and she's had twins by him too.'

'She's had twins with Raymond?'

'Not Raymond! The scabby looking bloke from City

Bakeries! Scabby looking twins apparently. They're not even divorced yet!'

Divorce? That's a new one too. Nobody got divorced in the sixties except maybe the odd Protestant, without telling us. In our world we were experiencing the height of Catholicism. The peak of its powers. We had more Benedictions and Hail Mary's going on than the Pope in Rome. Churches were full and confessionals were fuller. Divorce was not an option. It was a dirty word. Dirtier than some of the real dirty words. I hadn't heard of it. We were quite clearly taught that anyone who wasn't a Catholic was going to the bad fire anyway so divorce was the least of their worries. Also anyone who wasn't a Catholic was a Protestant. There were no other faiths groups mentioned or openly discussed. Glasgow, much like Ireland, was very much black and white in that respect, or rather blue and green. There were no colours assigned to Jews, Baptists, Methodists, Buddists or Muslims. They were all Protestants or 'Proddies' as we understood it. Simple if not enlightened. First new religions we heard of and accepted as not Proddies, was the Moonies and the Mormans, and the latter was only because of the Osmonds. Divorce if so trendy now even Catholics love it. Most eight year olds are now on their third step-parent. McDonalds global domination is down to one thing and one thing only. Single parent guilt.

My siblings know everything that's going on in and around the family, whereas I even had to make my example up just to illustrate the point about what hey know that I don't remember. I don't even have an auntie Brenda. I couldn't use a real auntie in case some of that information was accidentally accurate.

I don't know anybody in Glasgow anymore. I've now lived 'down south' longer than I ever lived there. That's a weird feeling. Whenever I go back to Glasgow I like to stand in the middle of Sauchiehall Street and wait to see if anyone recognises me. No-one ever does. But to be honest I don't think I would remember them anyway. My brother, Jim sees people I used to know all the time and they recognise him.

'I bumped into Frankie the other day.'

'Who's Frankie?'

'You know, Frankie?.. '

'No I don't think I do.'

'Yes you do, Frank! Frankie! You were at school with him."

'Oh Frankie!' I nod and smile.

'Yes, see?..You were at school with him. He says hello.'

Apparently I was at school with him, but I don't know who Frankie is.

But you see this is where I trip myself up, because just as I was making up the name Frankie for that little demo, at the very same time, I remembered Frankie Kerr. I was best mates with Frankie Kerr for a whole summer when I was about 13 or 14 - not entirely sure which. But I remember he helped me make a little white fence for our garden. He was a practical, jolly fat lad in the days when fat lads weren't ten a penny. But he didn't care. He was very cheeky and smiley and my dad liked him.

Frankie, streetwise beyond his years, was actually part of a family who were a bit rough. Rough in that they had form. By form I mean they were seen to be part of local gangs. His brothers I mean, not his gran or anything, though who knows? Frankie had that underlying sense that he could be a gangster about him, but he was obviously naturally too smiley and cheerful to be allowed to hang about with his more menacing brothers too much. With his portly figure and Crombie coat, Frankie at times looked like the star of a 'Clockwork Orange

- The Disney Musical'. Having a cute, smiley face is not good PR when you are trying to mug someone with a Stanley knife. It was clear though that Frankie had connections in the Glasgow underworld. How else can you explain how he got me my first ever job? The dream ticket! The one job every Scottish football loving kid of that age craved. Clearing up rubbish at Hampden Park after international football matches.

Word on the street, from Frankie, was that the job was virtually treasure hunting. Football supporters always threw money away, dropped Rolex watches and generally left gold dubloons lying around all over the place. And what you found, you kept. I can't remember what the pay was, but who cares? You made it up in treasure trove. Given that I never made my fortune in this way and that you haven't seen me on Dragon's Den as a result, you can guess that the reality of the job was not all our Frankie cracked it up to be. A group of us turned up at Hampden Park on a Sunday morning and were given a pair of those big rubber gloves, with shapeless fingers, made for someone with much bigger hands, and sent out with a bin bag each. It turns out that your average Scottish football fan is either very careful, or very skint. I never found a single penny. Not one penny! Just a lot of seemingly 'half-empty' cans of Tennants Export, but, trust me on this. It turns out that your average Scottish football fan does have two things.

1. A raging thirst for Tennants Export, and...

2. Quite a small bladder. Small enough to half fill a can of Tennants Export on a very regular basis over the course of 90 minutes.

Health & Safety would have a field day now of course, but personally I can't see the problem with taking a bunch of thirteen year old boys, with no parental permission, and sending them out to work for a whole day, with no break, and covering them in someone else's piss, for about 50p a day. The smell of stale piss always reminds me of my time with Frankie - that and white picket fences.

I can't actually believe that stale piss came up quite so soon. Bit annoyed about that. I jumped way too far into the future and right into the next book. I need to stick think this through chronologically don't I?

I wanted to write a beautiful 'Angela's Ashes' type story of my life that would begin with my very first clear memory from childhood. That first moment of awareness that I was actually alive and in this world. Not right at the point of birth because that would just be silly. Although I was born in a mental hospital in Lennoxtown just outside Glasgow and I always use that one as one of those little ice breakers when you meet new people and the conversation turns that way. It never gets the reaction I expect as inevitably, the other person had turned the conversation that way in the first place because they had a much better story to tell than being born in an 'actual hospital'. In my defence it was also a maternity hospital, so yeh even more boring.

Some people, I have noticed, write autobiographies as if, when they were five years old, they were fully aware of their surroundings and were already intending to write a book about it one day. I don't remember seeing too many kids in our street noting the smell of their mother's cooking or the colour of the wallpaper, or drinking in the sights and smells as they were dragged around the Galbraiths with their arse stinging because they kicked up a fuss about not getting a penny caramel.

'I'll just stop and make a note of this pain, mother and my inner reactions to it. It's for my book don't you know.'

'Stop dawdling you little bugger!' Smack!

'Oh, thank you mother. That'll make chapter two entitled,

"Why I hate my mother and keep a woman who looks like her tied up in my basement".'

Not quite as annoying of course as those endless TV programmes about the top 100 of everything and anything. Usually having a pop at the seventies and how bad the clothes were. You tell me how someone who is clearly no more than thirty, can tell us how we all felt stupid in platforms or flares? Well I will tell you this. We did not feel stupid in platform and flares. We felt stupid if we didn't have them! Because all our mates had them, so we wanted them too. My problem was that I always got the latest fashion about a year too late. So I actually did feel stupid as it turns out, but that's because I was actually there. Just doing it wrong.

That first moment I really remember will also be the first scene from the movie of this book. So it has to be good one. A classic moment of childhood romanticism that will leave them weeping before the opening credits finish rolling.

It is that point where the blinding sun slowly brings me into focus and I am cycling on my little trike just behind my brother Jim, trying to keep up. The sun is beating on the back of my neck and I can start to feel it burn. I am too young to know that by this time tomorrow I will be covered head to foot in Calamine lotion and walking like a burns victim, which I suppose is exactly what I am about to be. Anyway this is long before anyone gave a shit about a bit of sunburn. It's Glasgow. It rains a lot. We would take all the sunburn we could get. No rain today. This day is special and sunny, that's why I remember every detail. It's hard to pedal because the tarmac is melting. The tarmac always used to melt in those days at the first glimmer of sunlight. As soon as it did, we would proceed to dig it up with twigs or ice lollie sticks just for something to do, and to keep council workers in jobs repairing it again.

15

Kids today don't know they're born. Why sit inside all day staring at a screen trying to beat the living crap out of some beautifully proportioned girl with immense ninja skills, when there is perfectly good Tarmac to be ruined. I don't know if the summers were hotter then or the Tarmac was just inferior.

The smell all around is of freshly cut grass - isn't it always? Which is unusual because nobody had much of a garden to speak of. As usual my brother Jim and I are dressed in almost matching Sloppy Joes. (that's T-shirts to everyone else) We were very close in age, Jim being eighteen months my senior, so we didn't quite get dressed like twins but close enough that people kept asking. They don't ask now as, apparently, to the rest of the world, Jim now looks younger than me, but I hope to make enough of a point in this book about the fact that he is actually older, to stop anyone mentioning it again.

So there I am peddling like the wind in Jim's slipstream. I can barely make him out against the early evening sun which is blinding me. I am sure he is getting further away and I start to worry that I will lose him. He actually had a proper bike and in all honesty he probably is trying to get away from me. I couldn't ride a proper bike yet, so I had to pretend that I actually preferred a tricycle. My trike is obviously Jim's old cast-off so some of the paint is peeling with spots of rust showing through and that is probably ruining my aerodynamics. I can't keep up.

A combination of the blinding sun, blind panic and my exertions means that by now my eyes and nose are both streaming in equal measure right into my gasping mouth. I barely notice and gulp the streaming tears and snotters down with the smell of the Tarmac.

Tarmac is one of those smells that you can actually eat. I think everyone has a smell they can eat. If not then you might wonder what I'm on about, but I can't be the only one who eats the smell of Tarmac anymore than I am the only one who thinks Dr Peppers tastes like the smell of Germoline. Or am I? Regardless every time I smell Tarmac I have to gulp and swallow, so intense and lovely is the smell. Mixed with snotters it tastes pretty good too.

At this point I'm choking with the smell of the taste of Tarmac, snotters, and now some tears. He's losing me. I'll be lost. I'll never find my way home again. No one will even know where I am. I will die alone. Bear in mind we haven't left our street yet, but I am beginning to panic. The kind of blind panic that can bring on only one disastrous result at that age. Let be honest, at any age.

It usually happens these days when I'm in a car and late for an appointment.

I'm pootling along...nearly there..I'm a man. I've got my map. This is pre-Sat Nav, the greatest invention since sliced bread. Which it turns out isn't all that great after all, given that anytime we want a decent bit of bread, these days, we buy an unsliced one and slice it ourselves? It's taken us this long to realise it wasn't ever that difficult.

I've given my map no more than a cursory glance just before I left home and now all I have to do is follow my uncanny sense of direction. I'm a man. Probably didn't even need that cursory glance. I'm coming off the motorway into a town I've never been in before, but a road is a road and I am after all...a man. Unfamiliar territory now. A quick glance down at the map. I now realise I am not just a man, I am a man who cannot see up close any more without reading glasses. The map is useless. There is a beaten up white van driving up my backside. He knows where he's going.

'Yeh alright mate, try your brakes!'.

I keep that little bit of road rage to myself as he is obviously a working type man with muscles who knows how to fight. So I gesture to him that he is perhaps an irritant to me in the time honoured fashion.

'Wanker!'

Just out of sight but enough to make me feel better. That's taken my eye off the ball. I think I just passed my turning. He's all over my backside. I'll turn up next right..no, left...right!.. Bugger! He does too. He saw me do the gesture thing. Quickly turn again. Left. Lost him.

'Phew!'

Where am I? Why are the roads round here painted pink? It's a bus lane in a pedestrianised street. Pretend you know where your going. Old ladies are gesturing to me now.

I come out the other side without killing anyone, but now I don't know where I am. Then it begins. Oh no. No! Not that. Not now! There are rumblings. I can't stop. I have to hold on. I try to look at the map again but my panic worsens due to the fact that no matter how far away I hold the bloody thing, I can't make out a single street name. Why do they make them so fucking small? Shit! Traffic lights! Brake! I almost crash into the BMW in front of me and he knows it.

'Wanker!'

Me, not him. Well, he might be, but I wasn't in any condition to find out. Everything clenches now. Muscles tighten from your ankle to your neck like Precious Mackenzie trying to snatch and grab his own body weight. (Google him - a weightlifting genius but way too small to enter World's Strongest Man)

Nine times out of ten I succeed.

So just at the point where everything was about to end in a pile of shit, sweat, and snotters, my tricycle hits a bit of the melted Tarmac, that we had been digging up earlier, and I fly in extra slow motion over the handlebars onto the hot, sticky pavement to my doom.

I started to cry for real. Actually back then I would never cry. I would 'greet'. I never greet now. I was greetin' before I hit the ground in anticipation of the pain of a skint knee at best. I lay there for a moment upturned and greetin' when through the Sun's blinding haze, a hand reaches out to help me up. It was the first time I remember the touch of my mother's hand. It was soft and strong at the same time, which is actually true but Andrex have ruined that description for everyone. It wasn't very long though. She wasn't a big woman even then, though she looked big to me of course.

Jim was still peddling like his life depended on it and was half way to Bailleston by this time. (see map) He had in fact probably only made it to the end of our street, which was Denmilne Street in Easterhouse, a housing scheme on the east side of Glasgow. Most of the action takes place here, although the film director will probably have to fake this in a studio or use another street because, as you might expect, it isn't as big as I remember. It looks different. It's all flats and buzzer entries for young professionals who can't afford a proper flat or a proper job closer to the centre of Glasgow. I can't imagine what life would be like back then if we had to have a buzzer entry.

BUZZ.

'What?'

'Mum it's raining!'

'I know it's raining. It always raining. Let me know when it stops.'

'Can we come in to play?'

'Can you buggery.'

'We're wet.'

'You're not dragging your muddy feet all over my carpets.'
CLICK.

Carpets? It's not as if the house was all cream, fitted shag pile. There wasn't a carpet that touched a wall. All carpets were brought from your previous house whether they 'fitted' or not. You made them fit back then. The patterns were so busy you couldn't find a muddy footprint if you tried. Who transports a carpet these days? By the time I've left any house I've ever owned, I've been only too happy to leave the piss, mud, sauce and shit stained pile of disease ridden rug for the next poor sucker. But that might be because we all make the mistake of fitting cream shag pile now.

The point is we were always sent out to play and it took extreme circumstances to be allowed to stay inside to play. Living in Glasgow, rain wasn't ever seen as a very valid reason not to be out. So we were always out and when we got bored looking at rain, always trying to get back in again. Whoever had the most welcoming mum was always first on the list. It wasn't usually ours.

BUZZ.

'What!!'

'It's still raining, so we...!'

CLICK.

BUZZ.

'Muum'

'If I have to come down those stairs, I'll buzz you, laddie!'

CLICK

She never said that, but I bet if we had a buzzer she would have. Our actual version of the buzzer was to shout up at the window. Worked just as well. She never called me 'laddie' either. I'm getting all Highlands here. I must focus on my beautiful, but rustic beginnings.

Mum by now has me in her arms and after wiping every bodily fluid that I am, at that age, capable of expelling onto her permanent apron, is carrying me into the close and up the stairs. She will not drop me. I am doing that thing that kids do where they are not sure whether to cry anymore as the whole point of crying initially was to get the attention. Now that I have it there is no real need, other than to keep the sympathy coming, maybe get a biscuit out of it and get to play inside for a while. So I keep the odd bubbling going for effect. She sits me in dad's big chair and takes a good look at the carnage. I'd like to say now that I still have the scar, but in reality the damage was so slight she barely knew quite where to kiss it better. As mothers do though, she gave it her best guess.

'There you are, mummy kiss it better.'

The magical kiss of a mother somewhere near the area of pain works every time.

Roll the credits....I am safe now.

I am alive now.

I am...making all this up.

Everyone who has read Angela's Ashes will probably agree by now that I have not really captured the same mood. At this point I will confess I've never read it myself. I've only seen the picture on the front cover and assumed it was similar because the kid on there looks how we looked back then. So if this beginning is exactly the same as Angela's Ashes I can only put that down to remarkable coincidence.

You can see I wanted the big romantic opening. The page turning mood setter meant to make the reader wish they grew up in this cosy, comfy, okay from a distance, but a bit rough and ready close up, world.

But the point is I can't remember the first time I remember anything, which has sort of left me not knowing where to begin. We didn't even have trikes, bikes or scooters but to be fair if we had, Jim would have been trying to get away from me on his. My mum never came out in the street to pick me up in her Andrex arms. If we fell over in the street, we stayed there, 'greetin' until a crowd of mocking children gathered to laugh at you.

Maybe Julie Andrews was wrong. Maybe starting at the very beginning isn't a very good place to start. Especially if you don't really remember where the beginning was.

The period of actual childhood for me ran from around 1966 to 1971, Before that you're a baby or toddler, and who remembers that? Everything I remember about growing up mostly falls into the period of being aged seven and twelve. Maybe the odd event happened before, maybe after, but who knows. Not you. Certainly not me. Not without my diary that I should have kept. As for chronological order. Frankie Kerr was out of his time. He got me a job so that wasn't growing up, that was all grown up. We weren't there yet. There was growing up to do, even if we didn't know we were doing it at the time.

I could just pretend it all just happened one magical summer. Looking back it does feel that way sometimes.

CHAPTER 2

Dropping the Bomb

Perhaps one of the reasons we were kept outside to play was because when we were playing inside, we seemed intent on inventing grand ideas well above our station. Being outside in the rain kept us on our toes thinking only of survival, first from the rain itself and then from the real outdoor threat... bigger boys.

I am sure mums didn't give the bigger boys too much thought. Didn't realise the genuine threat that the bigger boy presented. Bigger boys are a species all to themselves. Growing older and actually bigger doesn't automatically qualify you to be a 'bigger boy'. I never became a bigger boy. I'm still not qualified. Bigger boys have a need to prey on smaller boys and feel good by making the smaller boy quake. I never felt the need to make another boy wet himself. I spent most of my childhood concentrating on not wetting my own pants. That said, there are upcoming scenarios that chronicle our attempts to be 'big boys'. I'm not proud of it. I didn't feed off it. But it did happen, so it has to be dealt with.

We spend so much time these days worrying about the worst possible outdoor threat to our children, if we allow them past the garden gate, that we forget that, for them, the biggest threat is still bigger boys or girls. Are bigger girls a threat to smaller girls? Does it work like that or are they all playing happily together and get bitchy much later. I don't know.

Regardless, we were sent outside amongst big boys with no protection or safety manual. Our only hope being that, if we encountered them, one of them might be a mate of a mate or distantly related to one of those many cousins we had knocking about. Being outside prevented any airy fairy ideas filling our little heads. Maybe our mothers knew of our potential to change or destroy the world, if we were left alone inside to think too much. But it could be that she just wanted peace to put her feet up with a cup of tea and a double digestive biscuit with butter.

Lets face it, kids are annoying.

But indoors is where our natural outdoors creativity became twisted. Whereas outdoors, a game with a stick would be over in a flash and onto the next stick. Indoors we looked for reasons...meaning...purpose. We had time. We had no natural predators inside. We had time to make things up.

The thrilling indoor football game of 'Subbuteo' was usually the source of inspiration for many a grand idea. Now, as I said that, I realised that I sounded like one of those eejits on those top 100 programme who mentioned 'Subbuteo' in a sort of post modern, ironic way because it looks primitive now compared to FIFA. I apologise. I wasn't meant to sound like that. 'Subbuteo' was great. Really great!

Jim and I did try the option of magnetic football once when one of us, (don't remember which) got it for Christmas. Magnetic football can be a bit frantic as you try to gain control of the metallic puck-like ball from underneath the table with magnetic sticks.

No, really kids!

We really were a primitive race in the not so swinging sixties. How we ever got to the moon, around the same time in man's history, is beyond me. The two things don't equate.

1. A powerful rocket that can propel man out of the Earth's atmosphere with all the relevant technology to keep him alive, get him to the moon, allow him to walk about a bit on there, transmit pictures back to Earth through sophisticated state-of-the-art communication equipment - then get him back again

through the Earth's deadly atmosphere landing safely within two miles of a big fuck-off ship....

Or 2. A magnet on the end of two sticks!

Is it any wonder there are conspiracy theories? We couldn't get a picture on our telly until the valves heated up and even then someone had to dangle out of the window with the ariel just to get a crappy picture with a big black line that kept going up and down and up and down. Drove you mad! We still watched though. You just had to keep bobbing your head in time to the lines.

Lord alone knows what the fighter pilots sitting around one day trying to get a picture on their telly, thought of the boss of NASA walking in

'Great news boys.'

'Here boss, you're tall. Hold this ariel'

'Lift your arm.'

'That's it. Nope, gone again. Stop movin' boss!'

'I cain't help it boys. Ahm mighty excited.'

'Why's that boss?'

'Because you boys have been specially seelected for a new programme.'

'We can't even get a picture on this one. Hang out the window will ya?'

'It's the space programme boys.

'What time is it on, boss? We usually get a better picture after nine o'clock.'

'No I mean outer space boys. We're going to the moon!'

'Fuck..off!!'

'Seriously.'

'In what?

'We're building a rocket right now.'

'Whose building this rocket?'

'Some of our top engineers.'

'Fuck...off!'

'You're right boys. Ahm just kidding wit' you.'

'You had me going there, boss.'

'I know. You shoulda seen your faces.'

'I damn near shit ma pants boss. That wasn't funny'

'Sorry Neil. Okay, so we're not really going, to the moon but don't be tellin' no one. 'We're just gonna take y'all out to the Nevada desert and film y'all like you were really there.'

'Why?'

'So we win the race.'

'What race, boss?'

'Seems there's a race with the Ruskies and we need to win it.'

'If them Russians ever find out we cheated to win a race, they re gonna be mighty pissed off.'

'No ones gonna believe it, boss.'

'Why's that Neil?'

'We cain't even get picture on this here TV, so who in their right cotton pickin' mind is gonna believe we can get to the fucking moon?'

Magnetic football didn't last too long for one simple reason. Before Boxing Day had even really got going, if it ever does, our dad had smashed the whole thing over his knee. I can only assume someone at his work had given it to him free as it did seem a tad wasteful.

The problem is that magnetic football is not a delicate art

and, other than outside, there is no games room that many parents these days feel the need to provide for their children. You don't need a games room!! Outside IS the games room!!... Sorry. It's just...don't you sometime just want to...? I mean who needs a....? Sorry.

Magnetic football is a frantic free-for-all. Sometimes the magnets work and sometimes they don't. Which isn't strictly true as a magnet is a magnet, and Professor Brian Cox would have a field day with that one. But you have to blame something. You have to really fight just to get hold of the bloody thing. Hence it caused much excitement and many an argument. I say 'many', but it obviously didn't cause all that many, given it wasn't long for this world. Jim and I fought and argued like two normal boys for what seemed like a couple of minutes but might have been hours. Long enough for our snoozing father to rise from his power nap, (although we didn't call it that back then) like a grizzly bear woken from hibernation two months early, to finally snap and bring Christmas festivities to a splintering halt.

We retreated back to the safety of Subbuteo.

Subbuteo never caused such arguments between us. That might be because we never attempted to actually learn the proper rules of the game. Had we done so it may well have caused similar arguments, but thankfully, we never bothered. We made up games and rules as we went along. In fact more often than not we would invent whole football tournaments, with all of the scores already decided, to the point where we knew which team was going to win and by what score in every game. All we had to do was make it happen and present the victors with the plastic replica of the original Jules Rimet World Cup trophy (available from the Subbuteo range).

These tournaments could take days though and we had to

prepare thoroughly. We collected a selection of large cardboard boxes from the local shops and fashioned them into grandstands with a bit of creative cutting and sticking. All teams not immediately involved in the game being played, were placed in the stands as spectators to create atmosphere. Actually they just had to look good. Jim and I created the atmosphere in the way of crowd noises and commentary.

The atmosphere was our biggest source of trouble, in a way, because so good were we at recreating the sound of a stadium full of 100,000 supporters and so carried away did we get, that we were often interrupted by our mum barging in at a critical point in the match just as a slow motion action replay of Peter Lorimer attempting one of his thirty yard piledrivers, was half way to goal.

'Hee haw, Hee haw!'

Mother attempted to re-create our sound.

'What?'

'Will you stop your bloody hee haw, hee hawing?!'

'We're not hee hawing.'

'That's all I can hear. Heebloodyhaw. We're trying to watch the telly and your faither is hanging out the window with the ariel as it is.'

SLAM!

It was akin to your mother barging in to catch you masturbating...so I'm told. It's a very personal and intimate thing. Jim and I were right in the moment and fully involved in making the kind of noises that you didn't even admit to your close friends.

You know I am still talking about Subbuteo, right? Course you do.

The most upsetting thing was that our crowd noises sounded

nothing like 'Hee haw' and it upset us that our own mother didn't appreciate our skills in this department. Even now that's how she remembers it. It actually sounded like 60,000 rampant Leeds supporters and another 40,000 traveling Liverpool lads. Our big cut off cardboard box could hold much more than your average stadium, even by today's standards.

It was always going to hit the bar, by the way. We knew that before it left his Bostick covered foot. Lorimer had no idea. Pre-determined. A bit like us and God if you think about it. Still worth a slow-motion replay though.

Anyone who has played Subbuteo will know that, eventually, all players will end up stuck to their bases with a sizable knob of Bostick. This supposedly table top game was always played on the floor in our house. Being knelt on was just an occupational hazard. It was Subbuteo's version of the modern day broken metatarsal. We could have played on the one table big enough to hold the pitch but that was perilously close to a slumbering dad and there isn't a team in the land who will be inspired to victory by 100,000 whispering fans.

The reason most of our tournaments involved English teams is as valid now as it ever was. Once you get past Celtic and Rangers, Scottish football isn't very exotic. And to be honest, as rampant Celtic supporters back then, we weren't over inclined to give Rangers much exposure, so we would use English teams and invent those tournaments where Celtic would happen to be in them and 'somehow' beat them all.

We did get involved in one real Subbuteo tournament at the local youth club, set up at St. Clare's school, once. We went in thinking we were the bees knees at this game thinking we knew it inside out, only to discover there were actual rules to it! Apparently you couldn't just move your men anywhere you wanted just to make the game more exciting. And commentary was frowned upon. We didn't last long in that tournament. Some kid called Simon, with a proper haircut, who probably still has all the teams in their original boxes with no 'Bosticky' players, (because he played on a specially made table top surface) and now sells them on Ebay, won it...I think. I'm not bitter.

I don't ever remember seeing rules when we first got it, but then I have to admit I am also one of those men who rarely sees rules...or instructions...or directions...or anything that might make life a little easier if we just stopped and looked for a second.

It's not a macho thing, it's just that asking for directions seems to just take the fun out of everything. Unless you are in the predicament I mentioned previously, (I'll spare the details again) Then it just might be considered valid to get you out a hole. But Sat Nav has solved all that and sucked the fun and danger out of travel.

Travel for us was all about 'The Bomb'. Whilst all around were unknowingly trying to ban it, we were riding it off into the sunset or wherever it would take us. No Sat Nav, no map, no seat belts, no room really. Our Bomb was our dad's grey Austin A30. I say grey as if that helps, but it might have been the only colour available. I didn't know or care who made it, we just called it The Bomb. It went like a bomb. It's all relative, as I'm sure any aficionado of vintage cars will be desperate to tell you, that the Austin A30 did not in point of fact 'go like a bomb' but could barely get up a gentle slope, especially with seven of us in there. Dad, mum, granny, Catherine, Jim, me and Paul. Youngest Stephen may even have put in a late appearance. The Bomb took us anywhere we wanted to go. The wind in our hair and a song in our heart. Okay that might be pushing it a bit as we were crammed in there like sardines with no air con and tiny windows. It got us where we had to go which was usually holidays in Saltcoats on Scotland's west coat Riviera. Saltcoats had it all. It was the playground of the western world. Cleaner swings, slides that didn't stick and those roundabouts with wooden floors. It also had the sea and I did like a paddle. In fact, still can't be at any seaside resort without dipping my feet in the water. Saltcoats did that to me. We would mix it up sometimes and go to Ardrossan half a mile up the coast. There's not much to see there now and I'm guessing there wasn't that much to see then. As soon as most of Glasgow realised planes had been invented, they were off to sunny Spain without a backward glance. Our furthest expedition was Blackpool and given it must have taken six hours or more to get there in The Bomb, you can see the attraction of supersonic flight.

The fantasy world of table top soccer was only really the beginning of where our imagination could take us if left to our own devices or allowed to play inside. Jim and I were joined in most of our imaginings by the third member of our gang,Wulllie Grimes. Wullie was the third only other living creature to experience our world as we did. Wullie lived in the next close a few yards away. Wullie, Jim and myself were inseparable best mates. His mother was also a little bit more laid back and might even been a bit hippy like. She may have been our closest connection to the other sixties, but we didn't really notice then. We just liked the fact that she would let us play inside more than our mum would. Whilst she was in the front room playing Buffalo Springfield, with flowers in her hair, we could shut Wullie's bedroom door to our world and plan our lives out. One particular day started as boringly as every other wet, dull day. We would spend half the day, drenched and begging to get inside and then when a parent, finally relented, we get inside we run out of games to play in what is slowly becoming a steam room as we dry off. Everything was cool and groovy. (sixties..see?)

Except it wasn't. It wasn't cool or groovy, was it?

The world needed saving. There were wars raging. The Ruskies were a real threat and we were on the verge of another World War only this time it would be nuclear and the whole planet would be destroyed. Countries were dropping bombs all over the place. Never had the world been so much on the edge of destruction as at that time in the sixties. The Cold War, The Cuban Missile Crisis, The Bay of Pigs, bread going up to thruppence a loaf. There was a feeling of impending doom.

If I had been one of those kids who watched the news and took note of all this in my little notebook for the novel that I would subsequently write, then I would have been as terrified as everyone else. I would be aware of a feeling of impending doom all around me.

'I am aware of a feeling of impending doom all around me.' I would write.

'It's almost four thirty. I have been home from school for over twenty minutes and yet mother still hasn't produced our tea. Wherever can she be? The feeling of impending doom grows within me and we've run out of jam.'

I'm only seven and the phrase 'impending doom' is one that I would use to describe practically everything. It says it all to a eight year old writing his memoirs.

'Maybe she's been hit by one of those Cuban missiles. Maybe the world is on the brink of nuclear Armageddon and no one has told us. My feeling of impending doom grows still more doomy and impending. All around there is the smell of cut grass. My senses are heightened. Why is it always cut grass? It's like an out of body experience, so aware am I of my surroundings and the sounds and smells. There is a distant siren. What can that be? Car alarms have not been invented yet. I move to the window dazzled by an unnaturally bright shining light as I do. It feels like walking into the very heart of the sun itself. I squint. Try not to look. I am aware of a shadowy outline of a figure below as I reach the window and stretch my full frame as far as I can to reach the handle of the window. I am just about to give up and the light grows ever brighter. Too bright. Somehow I make it and the window swings open and I see the shadowy figure much more clearly.

'It's mum on the way back from the shops with two heavy bags.'

'Mum, where's ma tea?'

'Make yourself a piece n' jam.'

'Ah cannae, we've run oot!'

'I bought some. Hurry up though, you've only got four minutes.'

'Four minutes?'

'Well, two now. There was a four minute warning, so I thought I would run to the shops to get some messages before there was a queue.'

'Warning of what?'

'Do you no watch the news?'

'I'm eight!'

'Just so you know, that isnae the sun shining, it's wan o' thone nuclear bomb things.'

'I thought it was unusual.'

'It is. The sun never bloody shines.'

'Nuclear what? Let me write that down.'

'Ah wouldnae bother son, we'll aw be died in a minute.. and a half.'

'I'm getting another feeling of impending doom.'

'Yur no wrong there son.'

'What can we do?'

'There's only thing ye can do in the time left, son.'

'What?'

'Make yourself a piece n' jam.'

A piece n' jam, or a jam sandwich to the uninitiated, was the answer to everything back then. We lived on them. Survived on them. And when hunger got too much and MacDonald's hadn't been invented yet, in this country anyway, a piece n' jam would do it every time.

But the world was in danger and we couldn't just sit around covering ourselves in jam.

You might guess that all that stuff that went on in the sixties never made it to our street. The whole world could really have been on the eve of destruction but we had no more idea about it than we did about the Beatles or Sputnik or JFK or even the fact that, at that time, Easterhouse itself was at the very heart of sixties gang culture with some of the most dangerous gangs ever known, roaming that housing estate at the peak of their dangerous powers. Their names were daubed on walls to mark their territory and it was those signs that often kept us in our place and stopped us wandering too far. Now I think about it we often had a feeling of impending doom if we strayed beyond where we felt safe.

I don't know where I was when JFK was shot, but I'm pretty sure I was in our street and jam was involved.

Our world was much smaller. It rarely went stretched further than half mile of where we lived. Beyond that was unknown and unexplored territory. If things were going wrong We didn't have Bono or Sting. All we had was Thunderbirds and Stingray.

So I don't know what came over us that day in Wullie's

bedroom. I don't know why we thought we could help, though to be honest we weren't thinking of joining the army, we just knew the world might need saving and were letting off a bit of steam - literally. We decided that day that we could make the world a better place. Our world still, not the rest of it. Still didn't know about it, still didn't care. This should have been an idea that we came up with, tried for a few minutes and then forgot about, never to bring it up again. Lord knows there must have been millions of those. None that I can give you examples of for the very reason just mentioned. This one stuck with us though. Stuck with us then and sticks with us even now. It was heroic. There may well have been an underlying knowledge and feeling that all was not right in our Narnia. That's how heroic thoughts and plans begin. All was definitely not right in Easterhouse and even kids of our age could not fail to notice that. It must have seeped into our being. As I said Easterhouse was at the forefront of gang culture in the country if not worldwide. You don't send a top celebrity like Frankie Vaughan onto the front line to organise a weapons amnesty if this area is not making headline news. Frankie came and did his bit, though I have no idea how successful he was, or if any of it lasted. Not sure what possessed him, but it was certainly a noble gesture and one that reminded us how dangerous the place could be.

'Gimme me the moonlight.'

'Gimme the knives and chibs and swords and guns.'

'And leave the rest to me.'

The Easterhouse remix of Frankie's big hit never really charted.

Although we were not aware of impending nuclear war, we certainly were aware that our world could be destroyed by the evil within it.

There was a ticking and violent time bomb of epic proportions that could go off at any time and it would have taken us all with it. We could at any time have been sucked into its blast. Easterhouse was not really the place to be making fancy plans. Or maybe it is the kind of place where you need your plans to be at their most fancy to keep all that at bay. We made it out without perhaps ever knowing how close we came to not doing so. All superheros are fired up by injustices in their own lives. Super villains too as it happens, but we didn't have the capacity to stay angry for that long or bear a grudge, so heroes it was. We must have thought we could help Easterhouse. We must have thought we could save it.

From what? We weren't sure. Not the gangs directly.

Bigger boys?

That's not saving the world, that's saving ourselves. But if bigger boys could be put in their place then surely the world would be a better place for our children and our children's children. Yeh, like we really thought about our potential to have children. We hadn't even found our first dirty book by then. We could suppress gangs of the future, by confronting the bigger boys of today. Who knew that when it came to those confrontations that we would usually lose? You don't think like that when you're formulating world changing plans.

Life changing plans as it turned out. The fanciest plan ever. We all loved comic books and every kid dreamed of being on e of those heroes with superpowers. But there were three of us, so we couldn't all be Batmen or Supermen. How do explain that in a crisis situation facing with a super villainous mortal enemy.

'Hold it right there, Supervillain. We're Batmen.'

'Which one?'

'All of us.'

'All three of you are Batman?'

'Bat men.'

'You can't all be Batman.'

'We're not, we're Batmen.'

'Why can't one of you be Robin?'

'Are we going to fight to the death or what?'

'Okay you asked for it. My new super weapon will destroy you Batman!'

'Batme...Oh never mind.'

Besides I was the youngest, so after Robin I would have ended up having to be Batgirl ands who knows where that might have ended.

We still wanted to be heroes, so we chose a different hero, one who was cool, one who lived in the shadows and one who didn't mind splitting into three. We had big plans to do noble deeds and feel good about ourselves. Hailed as heroes, our families would burst with pride at the mention of our names. Parades would be held in our honour and little old ladies would give us money for sweets. But our identity would have to be secret. No one could really know who we were or what we were doing.

We were in this together.

We swore to do good and help others.

We swore to fight evil, wherever we went, forever.

We were...The Daredevils!

CHAPTER 3

To the Batcave

We didn't have a costume. We didn't need one. Besides Lycra hadn't been invented yet. Let me clarify in case some smart arse researches more than I do.

I am aware that Lycra may well have been invented in the twenties by some industrial revolution type who went too far one day at some rubber fetish party. Or it was invented in the space race. That's always a good one. Again you have to wonder how this whole moon thing happened when scientists were busy inventing non-stick pans and cycling shorts.

'5...4...3...2...1 We have lift off!'

'Houston the egg has left the pan cleanly.'

The actual giant leap for mankind? Teflon!

I've just looked it up so don't stop reading to Google. It's really boring but coincidentally Lycra was invented the year I was born, 1959 by a team of scientist working in corsets...I mean working 'in corsets'..not 'in' corsets. Although who am I to judge? Now I think about it, I do remember it being on the news when I was sat in my pram sucking a rusk. I may have noted it in 'Baby's first novel' diary, realising at the time that it was a significant advancement in the world of fashion.

Anyway it wasn't invented in our world. I have no idea how the real comic book hero Daredevil had his costume made or what it was made out of. You have to wonder if these comic book artists knew something we didn't. They must have been pissing themselves when the first Batman and Superman TV programmes came along and they were all wearing big knitted woolly jumpers and tights.

'It's supposed to cling to the body and accentuate every muscle and sinew.'

'It does! I got my mum to knit it a couple of sizes too small.'

'Have you tried Lycra?'

'It hasn't been invented yet.'

'What if it rains?'

I think our awareness did stretch to the point though that wandering around a Glasgow housing estate in brightly coloured capes and tight jumpers with a big DD sign on them, might not have been the best survival technique.

We moved silently around, helping old ladies across roads whether they wanted to or not. A bit Scouty I'll grant you, but you have to start somewhere. They might have thought we were Scouts. I don't think we explained. It would have just got in the way of our work.

'Thank you sonny. You Scouts do a marvelous job.'

'We're not Scouts. We're Daredevils.'

'You're what?

'Daredevils! Double D.'

'What's a Daredevil when it's at home?'

'We're superheros.'

'Oh, can you fly?'

'No..not really.'

'Not really?'

'Not actually.'

'What do you do then?

'This.'

'Haven't you got costumes?'

You can see the problem. Just do the deed and move silently

in the shadows. No-one needs to know.

We would know.

We needed a place to lay low if ever trouble came knocking. It's all very well having actual homes to go to, but that isn't enough when you are out and about fighting crime, or what passed for crime in our world. It just doesn't feel right going home and sitting up in bed reading The Topical Times after saving the planet. You needed to stay on edge, stay in the game with your senses heightened. The Topical Times wasn't going to do that.

Jim and I spent many a night sharing a bed and a read of The Topical Times. We had to share a bed it wasn't like we had our own beds and choose to snuggle up in one. You did what you had to do. We had to share The Topical Times too. The Topical Times was, I would guess, the most wrongly titled annual there has ever been. It appears on the surface, to be the forerunner of Private Eye and makes us look like we were the kind of superheros who kept abreast of current issues and events in case they affected our share prices and had to sell off a slice of Wayne Manor. We weren't. The Topical Times was a football annual. I know! Football? Not even topical because it was an annual, everything is already old news. We would spend hours looking at page after page of black and white headshots of footballers for no real reason until we happened upon Terry Hennessey, who played for Leyton Orient at the time. Terry's only crime was to be balding in the days it was not quite so fashionable to be so. Terry's picture sent us into a fit of hysterics the likes of which you rarely experience in life. One of those tummy hurting, can't stop yourself, fits of laughter that never seem to subside. Poor old Terry had done nothing to make us abuse his image quite so much, but he is still capable of setting off the same reaction even now. That's all we needed, to be sitting in our beds laughing hysterically at a bald man, while the world went to hell in a hand basket around us.

You can see how reading The Topical Times distracts. Stay out in the world. Stay alert. To do this, just like Batman, we hid in caves. Okay not caves, dens. We had lots of dens over the years. We used to pride ourselves in making the kind of dens in trees and bushes that no-one could ever find. We have been laid in dens with people inches away from us without them knowing we were there - holding our breath. People with dogs even. God alone knows what we must have smelled of, if dogs didn't notice we were lying under a bush inches from them. We were not afraid to get down and dirty and most days would end with us having to scrub layers of what look like camouflage paint off our angelic faces. The average Commando would have been proud of us.

Most peoples idea of a den was finding an old mattress or a bit of corrugated iron sheeting and leaning that up against a tree. That's not a den, that being homeless. Batman did not go to all the trouble of digging out a cave under his house with his bare hands, risking it's very foundations, only to prop and old mattress up against the entrance so everyone knew where he was. He was stealthy. Bushes would move aside to let him in, or he would stick a waterfall in front of his cave. Mattress dens are more like the den of the supervillain, who makes a big show of where he lives. He wants everyone to know how much money he has and invariably makes the den the same shape as his head. We would mock such dens and their lack of imagination. Our dens had to be 100% undetectable to normal humans and dogs of course.

It's actually a shame, in one sense, we were never sent to 'Nam. The kind of cover we were skilled in creating would have brought many a war to an end much quicker. Either that or the Vietnam War would still be going on as the enemy just wouldn't be able to find us.

Although we lived on a council estate, it was on the edge of Glasgow so all around and just across the road was countryside. The area of countryside we had at our disposal was vast. At least it was to us.

There was one big area of wasteland backing onto the houses opposite that was our primary playground. This wasteland swept down to Easterhouse train station to one side and was bordered by farmer's fields at the other. At the bottom end of this was 'the longy' (an area of long grass) which had a ruined house in the middle of it which we obviously thought was medieval but was probably a 1940's shithouse. A road ran at the bottom alongside the canal. That road ran as far as 'the coalie'. (coal quarry). I say quarry. All I ever saw was piles of coal which we would of course, when bravery and stupidity combined, nick for our mums.

Obviously the Daredevils frowned on such behaviour but only usually when someone else did it.

It was this area where everything happened. This was our world.

I feel as if I'm describing Narnia or Middle Earth and maybe I should put a map in the front of the book so that you can get your bearings as things progress.

This land was magical. It had everything we needed most of the time. Some of the lands that we traveled to beyond it were just that little bit more mysterious and dangerous, provoking feelings of impending doom if I remember rightly.

But a good den was vital if we superheroes were to survive. We had to have somewhere to run and hide when the big boys came.

The best den we ever built, and the longest lasting structure, was right on the edge of the canal. We didn't really build much as it was mostly a tree overhanging the edge of the water. But we made it more secure and less visible from the inside. Snug as bugs in the proverbial we were. We could plan our takeover of the world and no-one ever knew where we were. No-one except the couple of cyclists who stopped one day right above us.

We instinctively switched to whisper mode.

Had they seen us? Were they stopping to beat us up? Were they big boys or adults? There is a different threat level for each. Could we swim the 'nolly' (canal) to get away or would we take them on like the superheroes we were?

Swimming the nolly was never a viable option. I couldn't swim. So we were stuck in the den, pooping ourselves. Which was ironic really because, as it turns out, so was the cyclist.

He was obviously out on a long ride and had been caught short with what can best be described as tummy trouble.

He hadn't seen us. He got off his bike and scrambled a little way down the bank and was now directly opposite the entrance to our den. He dropped his trousers and squatted. We didn't know what to do. We were torn by the thought of being discovered against allowing someone to shit on our doorstep and, of course, trying not to piss ourselves laughing. The latter won out. Just as Lance Armstrong was halfway to delivering his bombshell we could hold back no longer and all three of us burst out laughing.

Now, I don't know if you've ever seen anyone suck a jobby all the way back in, but it must take remarkable muscle control. That baby just disappeared right before our very eyes. It was better than any magic trick I've ever seen, or want to see again, if I'm honest. There are many things I am rubbish at recalling but that one burns my memory banks like a flashbulb on a tightly closed eye.

He called us all the little bastards under the sun, as if it was our fault, and scrambled back up the bank and cycled off. I always wonder how the rest of his journey went. He never returned though so our secret hideout was still a closely guarded secret. I think we would still be in that den now if we hadn't encountered a bit of problem. I am sure that we could have raised our three families, held down decent jobs and lived a good life just outside conventional suburbia to this day.

If it wasn't for that damn dog!

I suppose that's not very fair. It wasn't his fault. He was only a dog. We never even knew his name. He was a white 'Scottie' dog. Lovely he was. Cute. Nicely proportioned and obviously well bred. His only problem was that he smelled a bit. Again not entirely his fault, as he was dead.

I know it's not pretty and nobody wants to hear about a poor dead dog and you wouldn't be hearing about him now if his rotten smelly carcass hadn't floated into the best den we ever had and ruined it forever.

God knows where it came from. We didn't kill it. It wasn't our dog. Must have been out for a little walk along the bank of the canal and just fell in.

Sploosh!

Or was it trying to retrieve a ball or something and couldn't make it back to the side. But then what? It can't have been alone. So did it fall or was it pushed?

Isn't it funny how animal lovers get all squeamish about this kind of thing? Not bothered if it was a person, but a lovely little Scottie dog? Maybe I should change it to the carcass of an old granny. I'm making other stuff up, so I could just change that bit if it helps sell more books and doesn't alienate the entire animal loving fraternity.

To save time now I'll rewrite the dog bit using a granny and then the publishers can decide without having to come back to me later for rewrites when I've finished all this and can't be bothered.

(publisher - please use version as you see fit)

If it wasn't for that damn granny!

I suppose that's not very fair. It wasn't her fault. She was only a granny. We never even knew her name. She was a white 'Scottie' granny. Cute. Nicely proportioned and obviously well bred. Her only problem was that she was dead.

I know it's not pretty and nobody wants to hear about a poor dead granny and you wouldn't be hearing about her now if her rotten smelly carcass hadn't floated into the best den we ever had and ruined it forever.

God knows where she came from. We didn't kill her. It wasn't our granny. Must have been out for a little walk along the bank of the canal and just fell in.

Sploosh!

Or was she trying to retrieve a ball or something and couldn't make it back to the side.

But then what? She can't have been alone. So did she fall or was she pushed?

Oh..I have just had a thought.

Now that I have made the Scottie dog a granny, it has become blindingly obvious to me that the Daredevils, instead of just giving up and moving on to a better smelling den, should have investigated the mysterious death, Got to the bottom of it. This could have been our first big case...If only it had actually been a granny.

This was all pre-Taggart, so the world would have sat up and taken notice if a murdered granny floated into our den that day. We could have been minor celebrities. Obviously in those days without any stupid reality programmes to regularly appear on to build on our fame. It was all you could do then to get on Blue Peter. You had to have sailed round the world solo at the age of ten, or have written a complete symphony with your toes to get a Blue Peter badge and five minutes of fame sat on a padded bench beside a graffiti covered, gender confused tortoise.

But it wasn't a granny. It was a dog. A dead dog. And the Daredevils were out to save the world. Dead dogs were past saving.

So we moved on.

A new den. A new cave.

CHAPTER 4

Altar egos and Arch enemies

As I am sure you realise, we couldn't just wander around all day dressed as Daredevils and compromise our worth to society. Despite the fact that we hadn't really got around to making or wearing any costumes of any kind, we really needed the protection that an alter ego provide.

We had arch enemies who would love to know who we were. Okay they did actually know who we were, but they didn't *know* who we were.

Ronnie Black was the closest to an arch enemy we had. He even had an arch enemy name. He wasn't a 'big boy'. Big boys were an altogether different type of foe. Like aliens dropped into your world that you had to deal with, or you had to confront after being dropped into theirs. They were trouble, but a different kind of trouble. Ronnie Black was an annoying little shit who lived round the corner causing trouble right on our doorstep. He was the only blonde kid on the block in days when blonde kids didn't exist. Not evil albino blonde, just normal blonde. Except blonde wasn't normal. Kids are all blonde now. What is it they are feeding them, that they weren't feeding us?

Ronnie wore black to emphasise his blonde locks and stood on street corners, sneering and stroking a blonde cat, trying to look menacing.

The blonde cat bit is pure embellishment, nobody had cats. I hesitate to state that cats didn't exist, because they probably did, but I don't recall seeing one. That might be because of all the stray dogs running around scaring them off. Stray dogs were ten a penny.

People had dogs and then let them wander off anywhere they liked, without collars or dinner money. There was no such thing as a rescue dog. Rescued from what? From where? From who? They wandered the land experiencing the true meaning of sixties free love.

'Hey, Rover man...'

What? Nobody called their dog Fandango then.

'Hey, Rover man, you wanna like hang out with some way out bitches tonight?'

'Sure thing Fido, dude, I can totally make that happen. I am free all night long.'

'Don't you gotta be home to eat at some point?'

'Home is a state of mind dog, not a physical place.'

'I am totally down with that anti-authoritarian, anti-repressive sensibility.'

'We are not owned, we exist existentially, moving in and out of each other's consciousness with free will.'

'Is that why you don't got no collar?'

'Collars are the repression of the masses, Fido. Dogs and bitches have the right to freedom and sexual pleasure without social or physical restraints.'

'Ain't you hungry though? I'm always hungry.'

'I'm a lover not an eater. Love is my food.'

'Good, cos I'm hoping these bitches might be in the mood for love tonight.'

'Dude, this is a new world. You cannot tell anyone how to live their life no more. Lifestyle is an individual right and the result of free will and lack of oppression.'

'Only one style I'm thinking of...doggy style.'

There were no cats.

Ronnie would take great pleasure in intimidating me on my way to the shops and I often had to find different long-winded ways to get there as he lived right on Denmilne path on the direct route. He wasn't quite so brave when all three of us were there. I say all three, I do really mean when Jim and Wullie were there, given that I was stood well behind them and not much help if push came to shove, came to push, came to punch. It was a constant game of cat and mouse. Ronnie would make himself out to be threatening and I would run off or avoid him. He would appear on corners and from unsuspecting places taunting me with his powers of teleportation. He became a real nuisance and he knew it.

Then all three of us we would come across him on his own and a chase would ensue to rival any that Tom and Jerry would dream up.

Off he went like a whippet and we chased after. Up closes; down stairs; through gable ends; faces flattened with frying pans; anvils dropped on heads; into cars; off down streets, zig zagging to avoid pedestrians; onto tops of trains and through bridges; leaping into planes and dog fighting in the skies above; back to earth on parachutes; landing in speedboats zooming uo the Clyde; leaping onto horses like expert Indians; more closes; more running.

This happened every time we crosssed paths and should have had it's own music. I don't think we ever caught him, but these chases happened often enough to encourage him to finally mend his ways. We never made up or made friends, he would simply sneer from an upstairs window as we passed.

Philip and Robert Forsyth lived right below us and should have been good friends, but the older sibling Philip was a thorn in Jim's side. They weren't full on arch enemies, but annoying enough to keep at arm's length. Feelings between Philip and Jim were finally resolved in a single incident, (see chapter 5) set off by a discussion of the offside rule. After that there was little left to say.

So you can see there were times we needed to disappear. Live a different life where no one knew our secret and we could move freely. Well, as freely as you can in a long skirt.

Yes, Jim and I were, by day speeding, death defying, (apart from the Scottie dog) fearless superhumans, by night and most Sundays we were altar boys.

I don't really know why Wullie never chose that route, but I am sure it was because his dad didn't make him do it. Ours did.

His alter ego, consisted of just not telling anyone we were Daredevils. We should have thought of that. It would have been easier.

Being an altar boy had its moments though and when we look back now we always have a real pride at how good we thought we were. Back then men were men and altar boys were actually 'boys' who served at the alter of the blessed baby Jesus. Nowadays you get girls, women and more usually retired men. Now I am all for equality and jobs for the elderly, but where have all the altar boys gone?

Being an altar boy was like boot camp for superheroes. The art of 'altar boydom' taught you discipline, self control and pride in your appearance.

Made to walk upright with a wooden coathanger stuck down the back of your school jumper, Father Rogers was a stickler for posture. Try that one on a pensioner altar boy. They actually trained us for the job. Trained us! Look at the rabble that passes for altar servants these days, with their unkempt hair, dirty fingernails and trainers..and that's just the old blokes.

Dirty fingernails were the toughest obstacle for me. I am blessed, some say cursed, with the hardest fingernails known to man. Even to this day I have to use special professional elephant toenail clippers to cut my finger nails. You couldn't get those back then. Okay I know you probably could, but again, not in our street, with no money and the arse hanging out of your trousers, except on altar boy duty of course. The problem was they used to grow quite long as I had to get my Mum to cut them and hated the job of getting them cut.

I had to get my mum to cut them, as you ask, because they were very tough and I couldn't do my right hand with my left if you know what I mean. I know what you're thinking. I know you think I'm a big girlie whose mummy had to cut his nails for him. Well it wont help me then if I tell you that routine went on into my twenties.

They...were...very...tough!!

And as a result hard to keep clean. We were lined up for inspection before each Mass to check our fingernails and woe betide you if they weren't clean. Quite often mine weren't. I used to try and flash them quickly in the vain hope that Father Rogers wouldn't notice, but that was like Grasshopper trying to grasp the pebble from his master's hand before he was ready. A futile exercise.

Our costumes were long red priest like robes (the Satin) and a nice white, crisply ironed and starched, tunic (the Surplus), and black sannies - plimsols to the rest of the world). Fully kitted up with everything fitting properly, we were ready for action. It was a fine line between looking so good you could cut yourself and looking like a bag lady. You had to get in early and get first pick before someone else got the best robes or else your Satin was half way up to your knees or dragging on the ground, tripping you up on every genuflect, and your surplus looked like a dishcloth. Nobody wants to go into battle looking like you have already lost.

Our normal duties were mostly serene and serious. Lots of kneeling, lighting candles then blowing them out again. Too much staring at more gaping mouths than and ear nose and throat specialist as they waited for the Communion wafer to land. The odd taste of wine when no one was looking. We did actually once have a full scale battle on the holy altar of St Clare's Roman Catholic Church in Easterhouse. Our Tibet.

Unusually there were around seven of us on the altar that day. Two was normally enough for mass. Maybe three for Benediction, five for Stations of the Cross. This, however, was practise for an upcoming special event, probably a Confirmation. Confirmations or First Holy Communions always have that air of mass cult weddings. I suppose that's sort of what they are, just a mass wedding to the house of the Good Baby Jesus and his Dad.

We had more weapons that day than even Arnie could imagine. Right in the middle of rehearsal for the mass wedding, Father Rogers was called away. What urgent emergencies a priest has other than death - and by then it's usually a bit too late - I know not.

Anyway we were left scattered around the altar waiting for his imminent return. He seemed to be taking a long time and the tension was growing like a night in the trenches. Altar boys were getting twitchy. Nerves were fraying.

'It's quiet.'

'Too quiet, I don't like it.'

'Is he coming back?'

'Who knows?'

'Maybe he's left us 'ere. Left us 'ere to rot.'

'He ain't left us. He'll be back.'

'What if he don't come back?'

'He'll be back. He always comes back.'

'Not this time. He's left us to rot in this hell hole.'

'It's a bloomin' altar of the baby Jesus!'

'You know what I mean. We're done for.'

'Don't talk like that, you'll spook the young 'uns.'

'I don't care. I can't take it no more.'

'Snap out of it.'

'Don't tell me to snap out of it. This is my fifth Confirmation and they don't get no easier.'

'He's right. We'll never get out of 'ere.'

'Don't you start. Course we will. We always get out, don't we? Don't I always get you out?'

'Not this time. I can't waiting no longer.'

'Nor me.'

'Me either.'

We snapped.

Someone threw a hand grenade. It exploded right at my feet but with no effect on me other than to rile me enough to return the compliment. This one whistled over the flower arrangements and took out the enemy on the other side.

Before we knew it all hell had broken loose right under the crucifix. Machine gun fire rattled around with the familiar and fearful sound.

'Dadadadada..Got you! Yur deid!'

'No Ah umnae.'

'Ye'ur.'

'Ah umnae.'

No time to argue, or translate, I had to dive for cover almost knocking over the lectern. As I reached relative safety, I pulled out a knife. Now why I thought a knife was going to do any good when all around me were chucking hand grenades and simulating machine gun fire, I don't know. But it was a big knife and the fact is everybody loves to die a spectacular death at knifepoint. You ask anyone who has ever played Best Man Faller.

Best Man Faller is the ultimate test of how to die. It's easy enough to die a spectacular death at the hands of an explosive hand grenade, but the real skill is to die artistically from a knife thrown skillfully at great speed. It's all in the timing. My hope was the enemy would not be able to resist the lure of showing off an amazing knife death.

Now let me just say, at this point, for the benefit of the terminally politically correct and all those kids today who only know video game death. I am of course not talking of real dying. This is heroic, imaginative, fake dying at the hands of mimed weapons. It takes real imagination, outdoors away from a Playstation to throw yourself into the kind of certain death your own mother would be proud of.

'Did you see what he did there? That's my boy.'

'You could really feel the knife thudding into his chest, Mary.'

'Couldn't you just? You should see him being shot with a gattling gun. It just makes you weep with joy, so it does.'

'Has he always been this talented, Mary?'

'Oh Aye! Even as a toddler when he fell off the pram, he would somersault twice with a full twist before he hit his heid on the pavement.'

Whereas nows, it takes no great leap of imagination to

picture the kind of real death you are speeding towards. I think when I go I would like it be at the hands of a doctor who always wanted to be in the SAS. Just at the point of death after a long terminal illness, the doctors gather along with the priest, even though I don't want the priest.

'Once a Catholic always a Catholic.' He says.

It's a hard tag to lose.

They look solemnly on, then just at my last dying breath I leap up out of bed, drips and needles flying everywhere in slow motion. Doctor Khan pulls a six gun and Father O'Reilly releases a six inch 'Crocodile Dundee' type knife that thuds into my chest with the six bullets that the Doc has emptied into me. After much writhing and particular emphasis on each bullet, I finally collapse halfway down the corridor. I look up to acknowledge the onlookers. I try to speak but can only manage the kind of half sentence that all dead people do just to infuriate the living.

'I...just...wanted...to...say...that...I....'

I die...to rapturous applause.

That's how we should all go, but I fear for our future deaths as I can't really picture, in my head, how to die well from weapons of mass destruction. Maybe you need to get together with a lot of mates to make that work.

I've taken my eye off the ball and some junior altar boy is rushing towards me with a bayonet, screaming like a banshee. I wasn't expecting such close combat and to be honest, it doesn't really work as well, but he's young, he doesn't know any better. I pull the pin on the quickest grenade fuse you have ever witnessed and he is toast before he reaches the communion rail. But that was close. I'm going to need a bazooka to take a few of them out. I have to announce this of course so that they know what's in store. It's only fair as I've just made it up.

'Come'n make it, I've got a bazooka?'

The phrase "Come'n make it." is a magical prefix to any pretense set-up question, because it instantly, in the minds of both parties, puts the bazooka in your hand and renders the question pretty well rhetorical. The only way around this is to "Come'n make it." you have something better. But you have to think fast.

'Come'n make it, I've got a tank.'

'Well, Come'n make it, my bazooka has tank piercing shells.'

'Yeh but, Come'n make it, my tank's got a force field.'

'You cannae get force fields fur tanks.'

'Come'n make it, you can.'

'You cannae!'

'Aye..but...Come'n make it...you ..can.'

'That's no fair.'

Force fields for tanks? Someone always has to take it too far.

Just as the Battle of the Somme looked like getting out of control and someone was about to actually dig a trench under the altar, Father Rogers re-appears.

Not that we knew anything about the Battle of the Somme. Perish the thought that we should actually be taught any real history. I was more of a geography man anyway. I loved geography. Loved drawing maps with one of those pantograph things. A strange contraption and almost impossible to use with any degree of accuracy. Which is a bit worrying because I think, at the time, architects used them a lot. It was all I could do to trace a wobbly partial outline of Australia. I say 'partial' because most of it ended up being drawn on the big table as you could never really guess the scale of enlargement. Mother was not best pleased at finding the entire west coast of Australia engraved across her best table. God alone knows how architects built anything using one of these. I'm sure skyscrapers were never ever meant to be that tall.

'Aren't we designing bungalows, Quentin?'

A bit stereotypical on the name, I'll grant you, but they are architects and the ones with more normal names secretly wish they were all Quentins.

'Em yes we are, Quentin. This is a new style I have in mind.'

'It's huge Quentin.'

'Yes it is. It is pushing the boundaries, the envelope as it were, of where bungalows can go. Questioning the convention of the single storey dwelling and asking questions within the genre. It's ground-breaking innovation, Quentin.'

'You were using the pantograph again weren't you, Quentin?'

Bear in mind that an architect will never admit when he's wrong. Just build the fucker and blame the constructors if it falls down.

'Yes I was, Quentin, but in a new ground-breaking innovative way.'

'You've drawn most of it on your drawing board not on the paper.'

'I find drawing plans on paper such a restriction of creativity don't you?'

'I know just what you mean Quentin. It's just that it's thirty six storeys high and looks a bit like a wobbly looking map of western Australia.'

As for history though, I don't think we were taught the proper facts. History, as I remember it back then, was a bit sketchy. The Second World War was obviously too close to tell us about it or even yet call it history, so we were stuck watercolour paintings of Romans, Vikings and a smattering of Medieval living.

All of our battle experience came from American war films. The kind of films that now we like to scorn because America insists it won the war. We thought they did! So they did a good job of trying to convince everyone. Oh I know all about the Battle of Britain and all that but you can only hold your arms out for so long running around a field trying to kill your mates before it gets a bit boring and pins and needles kick in. So we didn't place much store by the Battle of Britain. John Wayne films and the like, were much more exciting. War was really exciting for us and I think kids today miss out on that because they are actually aware of the horrors of Iraq and that people really die horrific deaths. We shouldn't tell them. Lets the kids play.

I say they are more aware but they're not really are they? The difference now is they think war is like a video game. Visually exciting, lasts till about three in the morning and really hurts your thumb.

Father Rogers appears and we seamlessly end the war. Like in 'The Sting' where everything just folds away as if it had never been there and the poor mark (Father Rogers in this case) doesn't suspect a thing. I dispose of the machine gun in my hand with a scratch and a stretch. We only had standard issue machine guns apart from the gattling gun. We didn't know brand names like 'Oozi' back then. I think Father Rogers suspected something was afoot but he couldn't put his finger on it. If only nations could learn to end wars this way. As if they never happened. Just drop your weapons when someone catches you trying to be macho and brave.

'Come'n make it I haven't got a machine gun now.'

'Okay. Come'n make it my hand grenade turns into a tennis ball.'

'Great. Come'n make it my machine gun's a tennis racquet.'

'Right well come'n make it I had a tennis racquet strapped to my back all along instead of a bazooka.'

'Come'n make it we're just playing tennis then.'

'Okay. Come'n make it, it's my serve.'

'No. Come'n make it, its my serve.'

'My serve.'

'Mine.'

'You served first last time.'

'No, you did.'

'Didnae.'

'Did.'

'Didnae'

'Did."

'Right. Come'n make it, I was kidding about the tennis racquet and its actually still a machine gun.'

'You cannae do that. That's no fair.'

'Just did. Come'n make it, yur deid!'

'Come'n make it I was wearing a bullet proof vest.'

'Playing tennis?'

As undercover Daredevils, that battle had been a useful training exercise and one that would stand us in good stead the next time someone came at us with a tank that could potentially develop a force field.

'Come'n make it tank's huvnae got force fields.'

The time honoured 'Come'n make it' would be deployed instantly quashing any potential threat.

'Awright. Come'n make my spaceship's got a force field though.'

The world was changing too fast for us.

CHAPTER 5

All the King's horses

Like all the best superheroes we needed a butler. Not really a butler, more of a slightly weaker kid that we could push around and look good in comparison to. We would then train him to be at our beck and call to darn our costumes, if we get any, and test our killer moves on, if we get any. This would have to be stealth training, in that he wasn't aware the training was happening as we were still not ready to tell the world that we were fully fledged Daredevils. Others could have mistaken our actions for 'making stuff up' like kids do. It was more than that, at least we thought it was more than that. This was not 'Come'n make it' territory. This was the real deal. However, any show of 'theatrical creativity' would surely have rendered our macho powers over Egghead redundant. This is the 'bigger boy' period I was mentioning.

In our slight defence, he was sort of a mate. Not some random smaller boy that we felt the need to intimidate. It's just that it always helped to have one kid who made you look and feel brave. Not a pleasant personality trait, I'll give you that, but you don't think it through at that age.

Our 'butler' was John McManus or 'Egghead', as we so sensitively called him. That wasn't our fault really. His head was so obviously egg shaped it was hard to think of anything else to call him. I think he eventually got used to the moniker, though it may have affected him later in life.

It's not an original thought, but kids are cruel, aren't they?

Having the Big E hang around with us was my only real opportunity to feel a bit hard and cool. When he wasn't there my fellow Daredevils could easily summon the Dumbo scenario and have some fun with their perception of my ability to fly without the use of my arms. I had to keep the focus on Egghead.

'Yeh, but what about Egghead's big heid?'

'What about it?'

'It's...you know...big...like an egg.'

'He's not here.'

'He still has an egg like heid.'

'So what?'

'It's funny isn't it?'

'Not as funny as your ears, Dumbo.'

This then would normally escalate into musical renditions of popular flying related numbers, of which there were many, until I would retreat in tears with the potentially scary, but inevitably, hollow threat:

'I'm telling my mammy on youse.'

Nobody ever believed you would actually 'tell your mammy', and to be honest, if you ever did, you just got into trouble on both sides.

'I can't believe you told yur mammy.'

'Tell tale tit!'

'What did yur mammy say?'

'She spanked my arse and told me to stop telling tales."

You try to do the right thing and you end up in no man's land with your arse stinging. So doing the right thing with the Big E was a pointless exercise. I just had to steam in there and abuse him as best I could while no one noticed that they were supposed to be abusing me. I wasn't very good at it if I'm honest. My only real technique was to repeat was everybody else said, a fraction of a second behind.

'Ya big eggheaded freak.'

'Yeh...ya..big eggheaded freak.'

'Does your mother dip soldiers in yur heid in the morning?'

'Yeh...mother dip soldiers...heid...in...morning?'

'Have you got a lion stamped on yur heid?'

'Yeh...lion stamped...heid?'

'I just said that.'

'So did I then.'

'You're just copying me.'

'No, ah wusnae.'

'Aye ye wur. I just thought of that one about the eggy soldiers.'

'So did I. I just thought of it as well.'

'Bollocks! I just made it up.'

I'm sure at this point John McManus is patiently waiting for us to get in line and decide who gets to abuse him the most, or at least who wins creative control over the standard of the abuse. He was either a very patient lad, or didn't have anywhere else to go where he didn't get abused more. At least we didn't hit him. We would never do that. We were Daredevils after all and just trying to establish a pecking order so that everyone knew where they stood.

'I made it up too.'

'You cannae make up something somebody else has just made up.'

'I said it first.'

'No, you didnae.'

'I was just saying it when you said it.'

'Why don't you flap your big Dumbo ears and fly away?'

I went too far. I drew far too much attention to myself.

The Dumbo scenario will need an explanation and I will deal with it when the right time comes. It's an issue that needs exploring, but if I go there now this whole tale might twist and end up the bitter memoir of a supervillain who was called names just once too often and planned to destroy the world from his cavernous ear shaped flying machine.

All this isn't really helping the whole Daredevil superhero persona, so I'd better stop being so factual and make up some bits to make us sound more heroic.

When John McManus was ten, he contracted some sort of, oh I don't know, kidney type trouble from an addiction to milk or...broken biscuits. One of those. We were simple people back then and would have happily accepted either of those explanations, or even a plausible one. Anyway he needed a new kidney which Wullie, being the perfect donor happily obliged. Jim and I had both removed our own kidneys, with a sharp stick, in readiness but it turned out that Wullie's kidney was just fine, so we posted our kidneys to the local orphanage, who we heard were very grateful, but pointed out in a letter some weeks later that their orphans had all the kidneys they needed. It was parents they didn't have. We should have sent them to a local hospital's children's ward. You just don't think it through at that age. This was of course way before Children in Need. Oh, if only we had that then. The good we could have done in the name of Children in Need. We wouldn't have donated any more organs I don't think, but our charity work could have taken off big time.

I say charity work. The real extent of our charity work was a scam so devious and complicated that it almost managed to convince us we were doing the right thing at the time.

Just when I am at the point of re-dressing the balance in favour of good, I am sucked into a real story of pure cunning and greed. Okay, I'm going to tell you, but I want you to keep picturing Egghead's kidney in your head the whole time. Visualise the kidney. Do you have it in your head? Can you see the actual kidney being placed into his body? Good.

Because our big charity project was actually to con my dad and all his workmates in a charity scam. It didn't start off as a scam. It wasn't meant to be a scam. We were given one of those football cards to raise money for our local boys football team, where everyone picks a team, pays a pound and puts their name on the card in the box. Whoever wins keeps most of the money with some going back to the charity. In this case it was the football team we were somehow playing for at the time. Not sure how we managed that, but I will come back to our sporting career later.

The winning team's name is hidden under a padded silver strip at the top of the card. A strip so secure that no-one could ever know what was under it. Try shining a light through. No chance. Try looking through the back of the card. Not possible. This strip in impenetrable. It was, at the time, the pinnacle of security in the sixties. It seems strange now in this world of holograms and contactless chip and pin, that one silver padded strip could protect the secrets of the universe. But it could. It was the most trusted security measure of the age and, bearing in mind the millions of pounds of charity money at stake with hordes of similar children to us running around with the exact same cards, It had to be good. It had to be James Bond good. And it was. It was the kind of device Q would give James with the secret code to nuclear destruction hidden under it and a stern warning.

'This security device is state of the art, Bond.'

'Yesh Q. I can shee that.'

'You must never let it get into Russian hands.'

'Yesh Q. I will keep it shafe. How can it be cracked Q?'

'It can't Bond. It must never be cracked or it will mean the end of the civilised western world, Bond. Total and utter devastation. A new Ice Age.'

'Ice Age 6?' *(Apologies if they have made several more Ice Age films since and this dates the book for you. Think of it as a period novel.)*

'No Bond, not another cartoon in the already overdone franchise, I mean the complete destruction of the entire planet. It's all down to you Bond.'

'Yesh, Q. I get the point.'

Everyone believed in the silver padded strip as a system. My dad believed. His work mates believed and for a long time we believed too. Of course we wished we could see under it because who isn't tempted to glimpse the forbidden. That is why we rely on the system to keep temptation from our minds. We are only human after all. If God had hidden the apple under a padded silver strip all this could have been avoided. By this I mean evolution, the ascent of man and life as we know it. Easily avoided. We would all still be naked in the garden eating unripened pears from one tree. So you can see, this system worked just perfectly.

Unless you just peel the silver strip back and had a look.

Yes, folks you just peel it back and stick it down again. To be fair, there was no way of actually knowing if it would stick back down, so peeling it back was risky business and required all the nerve and steely determination of a bomb disposal expert.

'Just do it!'

'I'll do it.'

'Ahm doing it. Shush!'

Beads of sweat formed on Wullie's brow and begin dripping onto the card. He had to act swiftly or the card would become soggy and appear tampered with. One or two fake names were already on the card and written in normal Biro. If the water droplets reached those it was game over. The soggy ink would smudge and run and no one would believe the fake names were real. They weren't of course, they were fake. In the movie version, this scene would take bloody hours and something would happen to jolt an arm, or make him drop the device down a crevice with no time to spare. The reality is we were getting bored waiting for Wullie to get on with it so Jim made a grab for it.

'Right that's it, Ah'm doing it!'

As he grabbed for the card, Wullie pulled the strip.

It was done. There it was in black and white. We all stared at the name. Albion Rovers. It wasn't Albion Rovers and in an *addendum* to this book Jim will remind me of the actual team name. But for now it is Albion Rovers. There was no going back now. It was done. Unless it wouldn't stick back on, then we were all pretty well fucked. Couldn't sell the other names. Couldn't take it back to the football club with no names filled in and the strip removed. We would have to leave the country. Trouble is, we didn't know how to get to Brazil. You don't do you at that age? I could draw it. I could scale it up onto the kitchen table with my pantograph so I knew the geography of Brazil and where it was in the world, better than most Brazilians. But which actual direction do you start walking to get to Brazil? You can't get a bus, unless you ask your mum for money and that wasn't going to happen, so you are walking. I doubt we would have got further than the other side of the canal until we were hunted down and sent to bed with no tea. Which to be honest, if it was a Monday, would have been a blessing as it was always mince and tatties on a Monday. God, I hated mince and tatties on a Monday. It wasn't Monday.

'Stick it back! Stick it back!

'Ahm doing it. Shush!'

It stuck! The scam was afoot.

Can I just remind you at this point of Egghead's kidney, which even though not even real, still comforts me somewhat. I'm sure we would all have donated if he had just asked. You see, the thing is, this con still riddles me with guilt to this very day. How could anyone do that? How could such seemingly innocent and well meaning children rip off their own father to that extent? I'm only asking the question. I don't have the answer. I only have the burden of guilt that I wear like Jacob Marley's chain.

The look on my dad's face, after selling at least 90% of all the names on the card, when we revealed - with a lot less fuss than before - the name Albion Rovers under the impenetrable silver padded strip, was one I will never forget. Revealing that one of our 'teachers' had one the prize, he was purple with rage. How could that be after all the tickets he sold? How could that be? This wasn't the moment to tell him how that could be. This was the moment to shrink to the size of pea and crawl out under the door. Interestingly, he never suspected foul play. He had as much faith in the security of the silver padded strip as Q had.

I can't remember what we did with the money. I'm sure it was only a pound. Not quit enough money, even in those days though, for three terrified kids looking to make passage to Brazil on the next steamer. In the end we probably bought sweets with it. Your average modern child would wonder why you would spend it on something so trivial that you can get hold of everyday anyway.

'What a waste of time' They would say.

Actually they would say 'What a waste of time, innit?'

But you didn't get sweets everyday. At least we didn't. We didn't get sweets every other day. We practically never got sweets. Is it any wonder really that we were driven to such lengths for a sweetie fix?

At last, justification of our deeds! It was all their fault anyway. They made us do it. It was our parents that made us what we were. I think Wullie did alright for sweets, if I recall, but we didn't. Now I think about it Egghead was always first out to the sweetie van buying packets of crisps, Mars bars, Irn Bru and penny caramels. No wonder he had trouble with his kidneys.

We had regular sweet vans that came around the estate. Like ice cream vans, but without the ice cream. Ice cream vans were a much rarer occurrence, and if Scottish films on the subject are to believed, all business fronts for selling drugs. I don't think our sweetie van was that. If it was I didn't notice, but it might explain my addiction to sherbet dib dabs to this day.

Don't get me wrong, we were always sent to the van when it came around. But it was always to buy fags for mum and dad. 20 Embassy Tipped for mum; 20 Senior Service for dad. When they had the money, on rare occasions, they allowed a little extra to buy three ha'penny caramels. A small chocolate covered chew. Nice enough in their own right, but a social stigma in this case. The thing was there were three of us. Jim, who you know, and Catherine our elder sister. The three ha'penny caramels amounted to one each!

We never did pluck up the courage required to tell mum or dad to stuff it and not bother. No one is that brave. So each time it was offered, we took it. The trick was not to look as if that was all you were allowed to buy. The trick, was to make it look as if you were just spending the change from the fags in a cavalier fashion.

'Oh tell you what, just chuck in three ha'penny caramels as well, mate. What the hell. Bugger the change, eh?'

'Would that be that the same three ha'penny caramels you bought last month?'

'I happen to quite like ha'penny caramels once in a while.'

'You never buy anything else.'

'Oh really? Well here's a whole pound that I have just acquired. So that'll be four hundred and eighty ha'penny caramels please.'

Egghead recovered from his kidney trouble, thanks to our transplant and the wonders of modern....yeh..yeh...whatever. What he needed now was training. Commando style training. The kind of training where he wasn't really aware it was happening and we didn't have clue what we were doing. The kind of training we were expert at. Not really the definition of 'training' I'll grant you. It is more about taking the geeky kid along to make us look good. Beside we had read many Commando comics by then and Egghead was reading proper books, for some reason. Commando comics taught us basic German, such as 'Gotten himmel'...and...and...well as I said basic German. The Germans weren't exactly winning in those comics.

Being fully at one with nature, as we were, we sniffed the air, checked our internal seasonal clocks, and knew instinctively that a window of opportunity was open and it was time to answer nature's call. (not that one) It was an in built drive. Not something we could control. Or possibly we saw some other lads doing it and just joined in. Regardless of how it came upon us, it was time for Egghead's first field trip. We had planned a trip to look for bird's nests, burgeoning with newly laid eggs, and the butler was coming along. He rarely came on longer trips with us and to be fair I don't think he expected this one to be that long or he would never have agreed to come along.

We donned our ripped jeans and melted anoraks and Egghead was suitably attired in oversized khaki shorts, school satchel and pith helmet ready for his first trip to the Equatorial Rainforest. I might be being a tad mean to Egghead's memory here, but as that is in keeping with the whole tone, we'll not worry too much about that. It's how I picture him, I can't help it. We weren't heading for Brazil (yet), being superheros we were on a dedicated mission to save the more local bird's eggs from gangs of marauding egg stealers, by collecting them ourselves. Egg stealing, or collecting as everyone called it, was rife and conservation was unheard of. Well unheard of like Lycra was unheard of. We hadn't heard of it. I am sure many conservation groups started back then telling the world that every species was dying out and we only had four minutes to live. We were out saving the world for ourselves, in our own special way.

Egghead followed loyally at first, his limp limbs swinging at his side not really knowing how to walk in a cool way. He sort of limped and stuttered along behind. Just past the canal road, the road becomes a bit countrified on both sides and there are rows and rows of hedges...and rows and rows of hedges. We could easily have given up, but given our main search was for the nest of the very common hedge sparrow, we knew that we might be on the right track. At last we struck pay dirt. A hedge sparrow's nest. With a quick furtive look around, presumably to check no sparrows were watching, Wullie nabbed the eggs from the nest and handed them to Egghead, who placed them carefully into his satchel, and now had to walk more gingerly than ever for fear of breaking them. Yes, that's right he took the eggs out of the nest. It sounds bad now. For some reason it didn't feel bad then. We were collectors, inquisitive about nature. Besides, what harm could it do? Yes, I know that now!

I think it was the desire for something a bit more exotic that led us to some taller trees. Lets call it a forest, as it seemed like that at the time. But it was only a clump of trees. I am pretty sure that Red Riding Hood's granny never, in reality, lived at the other side of forest. It was just a clump of trees. But there high up in this tree was our ultimate goal. Crow's nests, and the potentially exotic addition to our collection of two sparrow's eggs. That was when we encountered our first big obstacle. Have you any idea how high they build those bloody things?

Don't get me wrong I know this now, but this was a complete revelation then. We were superheros of course, but not the flying type. We spent some time trying to persuade Egghead that it was a rite of passage and part of his training to climb all the way up there to steal an egg, and anyway most of the eggs were like brothers to him.

'Training to do what?'

'Climb trees.'

'I don't want to climb trees.'

'But you need the training.'

'You climb it.'

'We don't need the training.'

'Good. So you can climb it then.'

'We *can* climb it, yes.'

'But you need the training.'

'I might die.'

'Or learn a valuable skill in your training regime.'

'What training regime?'

'To be our bu...'

'Don't say it. He won't get it.'

'...Buddy...Our buddy.'

'I thought I was already your buddy.'

If anything we had been too stealthy. He thought he was our mate. Never frat-anise with the help. Rule number one.

Hold on there a cotton pickin' moment. Did I say 'steal' before?

No!! I meant we were saving the little birdies. We wouldn't take the eggs. No, that was what the bad boys did. Let me re-write the previous passage for more accuracy. My apologies for the errors in the previous version.

"At last we came across a hedge sparrow's nest and Wullie nabbed the eggs from it and snuck them into a little bag and handed them to Egghead, - FOR WEIGHING AND TAGGING - who now had to walk more gingerly than ever for fear of breaking them - BEFORE THEY WERE ONCE MORE RELEASED INTO THE WILD."

Oh yes, we were tagging and weighing long before Bill Oddie got his hands on a couple of tits in a bush. What we didn't have though was enough rope and tackle; persuasive powers or the balls to climb those trees for a stupid bloody egg. The crow population has of course boomed because of our lack of ability to get anywhere near a crow's nest. I often feel guilty at the annoying rise of the crow population. With a bit more courage, skill and heart we could have curtailed their rise. However, without the option to travel to OZ, befriend Dorothy, follow the yellow brick road and seek the Wizard's wisdom, it wasn't to be. By the way anyone had the opportunity to be a friend of Dorothy then without people getting the wrong end of the stick.

We stood looking up for a long time until our necks ached. Waiting for one of us to admit defeat, turn into Tarzan or for the tree to fall. The crows were mocking us, like crows do. From on high. Cowards. Egghead was panicking. He wasn't allowed out after dark. His dad would go mental if he wasn't in before dark. It wasn't dark, but it didn't stop him panicking that darkness was a possibility. I think his parents must have been ahead of their time, because no kid seems to be allowed past their garden gate, never mind allowed out after dark these days. His dad was a new breed obviously. Egghead's nerves gave us all the perfect excuse not to attempt the climb. I knew we weren't going to climb. Jim knew we weren't going to climb. Wullie knew we weren't going to climb. Egghead didn't need to know, he just needed to think we could if we wanted to. Definite need to know basis. He didn't need to know that I had never climbed a tree in my life. Of all the life stories littered with boys climbing trees; falling out of trees or even breaking arms falling out of trees, this is the one with no tree climbing in it. Climbing trees was scary. I was much happier at hedge height. Man wasn't designed to climb trees. Okay, I get the whole monkey/ape connection, and they do seem pretty good at it as a rule, but I think my gene pool must have come from a much more timid monkey lineage. I don't really believe all those tree climbing exploits anyway. Apart from coconuts, what's to be gained?

We gave up and turned for home with an impressive haul of two hedge sparrow's eggs.

We turned for home only to wish we hadn't.

As we turned we were suddenly faced with a shadowy figure right in front of us. A dark, hooded figure in the days before hoodies even existed. Hoods existed, but we didn't feel the need to give people who wore them a name. Every duffle coat and anorak had a hood, so it didn't seem all that special and I don't recall the sixties being particularly noted for the fashion accessory of the hood. Not in Glasgow anyway. It is so wet there, you look a bit ridiculous without a hood.

There he was all the same..our first hoodie.

Then another...

...and another.

This was scary. I am now picturing mist all around, although I am pretty sure there was no mist. There will be mist in the movie version, even if I don't picture it here, so I may as well picture it now. Wullie immediately reverted to his 'hamster hands'. He had a default position, probably foetal, where in times of fear or doubt his hands covered his mouth like a nibbling hamster. It was a sure sign things weren't right. It was never a pose that I looked forward to as, being older than me, I was hoping for a take charge, hands on hips, kind of super hamster pose. So, we were in trouble and Hammy Hamster was going to be no help.

Looking less like hoodies now and more like Deatheaters from Harry Potter. I have no idea how JK describes Deatheaters in Harry Potter books, or lets be honest, any desire to go read them to find out, but it can't be far off - 'a bit like misty, big boys in a forest at night'. Our own big boy period went up in a puff of bravado. And if you have ever smelt bravado, you will realise precisely what just happened. Because right there all around us...were actual BIG BOYS. They led the conversation.

'Awright?'

Jim replied with some bravado left.

'Awright, mate.'

'Mate?'

I can't believe it. Jim went with 'mate'. Who goes with

'mate' in your first encounter with a Big Boy in a dark and creepy forest? Jim was always a bit more courageous than me. I say ' a bit more' I mean a lot more.

He was a good fighter. I truly believe that if he been given the opportunity to see the film Rocky, he would have gone down that route. Inspired by Rocky's courage, emotion and Jim's love of beating up other kids, it would have been a potent mix. I can see him now with big woolly boxing shorts with a secret 'double D' sign sewn into the corner and his name, written indelibly on a label, sewn on the inside, in case it got mixed up with the other boxers in the changing room. A bit like Lycra, you couldn't get those big shiny shorts they wear now. He would have been 'The Daredevil'. Undefeated champion of the world. He would have needed a bit of discipline instilled in him by Rocky's trainer. Jim's technique was to pummel and pummel until someone dragged him off his poor unsuspecting victim. He didn't start these fights. They weren't unsuspecting in that they weren't spoiling for a fight. They were unsuspecting in that they thought, understandably so perhaps, that all fights between kids involved a lot of pushing and shoving that sort of led nowhere.

'Come on then.'

'You come on.'

'Yeh? Well, you come on.'

'I'll come on if you come on.'

'I'm coming on.'

'Right, well. Come on!!'

'You come on.'

This can go on for literally hours, with any nearby friends caught up in the 'frenzy'. Jim wasn't a patient person and he had a hair trigger.

'Come on then.'

'OK.' Jim just went for it. BAM...BAM...BAM...BAM....
BAM.

Everyone, at that point, usually panicked.

'Come off!!..Come off!'

I mean it was effective, but brutal. I have seen him break
his hand on another kid's jaw. I'm not proud of it, He is not
proud of it. I am just saying. He broke his hand on another
kid's jaw!! (yes it was Phillip) Maybe his lack of discipline
would have been more suited to cage fighting. All of this is a
moot point as there is one thing about Jim we didn't know at
the time.

Jim only grew up to be five foot six and a half. The big boys
in the cage fighting ring would have killed him.

'Who are you calling mate...mate?'

Good question I thought. Jim had the answer.

'Aren't you Billy McDermott's brother?'

Brilliant, we're saved.

'Who the fuck's Billy McDermott?'

Oh, maybe not. I tried to help.

'We're the Daredevils.' Did I just say that out loud?

'The what?'

'Are we?'

I forgot Egghead wasn't on board yet.

Wullie dropped his hamster hands to explain clearly.

'We are. You're not. You're our butler.'

'Butler?'

'Butler?'

'Butler?'

'Butler?'

'Butler?'

'Butler?'

Everybody said that. It's not important in what order. Wullie explained fully.

'Like Alfred.'

'Who the fuck is Alfred?'

A confused and annoyed Deatheater was starting to think we were taking the pish.

I tried to stop myself explaining. I really did.

'Please don't say Batman. Don' t say Batman. Don't say Batman.'

'Batman's butler.' I failed.

'Oh aye, him.'

Phew! I then thought a bit more hierarchy establishing would help make me look cooler than I was sounding. I'm not proud, but it was dog eat dog...So I used his name.

'Egghead is our butler.'

'Eggheid?' He translated.

They pished themselves. We joined in and pished ourselves. The only one actually pishing himself was the silently humiliated Egghead. The main Deatheater broke off.

'That's fucking cruel.'

'His heid is shaped like an egg.' Deatheater two was still amused.

However Deatheater one had noticed something.

'Look at the size of his fucking ears though.'

'Fucking Dumbo.'

Shit! I was rumbled. They pished themselves even more.

Great, now I was bottom of the heap. I HATE that film. Even Egghead was thinking about joining in. Jim's brotherly instincts were twitching and I think we were on the verge of carnage. Calling me Dumbo was his thing. Strangers weren't allowed. Suddenly Deatheater number two spotted the satchel with the eggs and we were saved, for now.

'You collecting burd's eggs?'

'Do you want them?'

'What are they?'

We offered them in return for our lives.

'Sparrows.'

'Sparrows!??'

'Sparrows!??'

'Sparrows!??'

Again all three Deatheaters said that with the same amount of mirth, disdain and incredulity. It's not important in what order.

'You should collect starlings or rooks eggs.'

'They're too high up.' I explained

'Fuck off.'

Apparently not. I really wasn't helping us to sound macho here.

'Any wanker can get sparrow's eggs. We've goat hunners.'

It wasn't the time to get smart and agree. They may not have been as dumb as they looked.

'Want to see a kestrels' egg?'

'Sure mate.' Jim replied with ever friendly banter, but I still thought he was pushing it. Lowly sparrow hunters don't get to call big game kestrel hunters, mate. Not yet.

Deatheater three pulled out an exotic looking egg from his pocket. I had no idea if it was a kestrel egg or not, but it was in our best interest to be suitably impressed.

'Wow!'

'Wow!'

'Wow!'

Everybody said that. It's not important in what order, except Egghead who was becoming more and more uncomfortable. He had to be prodded.

'Wow!'

All of this bonding over bird's eggs is, I realise, a bit unsettling seen from the perspective of the 21st century, with the sparrow population now in such decline and being blamed on sparrow hawks, who must have been thinking.

'I'm pretty sure we didn't eat all of them! I know it's in our nature, but we're not pigs.'

Nobody has thought to ask us and we have kept our heads down, till now. We genuinely thought we were doing no harm to the species. We were collecting, like Darwin collected butterflies and stuck pins in them. The world was there to be discovered, at that point, and now that it has been discovered, we are not allowed to stick pins into it. Or pull the wings off it. Like Wullie's pet bee.

It was a pet! No point in having a pet if it flies away as soon as you open the jar. So what Wullie, and many others, did was pull its wings off. This is getting worse. There was only any point in pulling the wings off a 'yellow nose' bee which has no sting...and now no means of escape. Normal bees would, of course still sting and you could hardly blame them. So they were no good as pets. You had to keep those in jars until... until...until...'You tagged them and released then into the wild.'

Now that bees of the world are also in steep decline, this is starting to look really, really bad. But I refuse to sugar coat the past just to make us look good. Everybody did this kind of thing. Blue Peter painted tortoises and chimps were dressing up to sell tea!! It was a different world.

For us, the eggs were saving our skins, if not the sparrows.

'Kestrel, mate.'

'Want to buy it?'

It's not exactly 'Kes' either is it? Boy befriends kestrel who teaches him healthy, if gritty life lessons. Or boy steals kestrel's egg and puts pin holes in either end, blowing out the insides and destroying any chance of life young Kes ever had, leaving boy with useless, but pretty, hollow egg that he can sell for sweetie money.

'We huvnae goat any money, mate.' Jim confidently informed them.

'Prove it.'

Oh bloody hell, now we were being robbed. I knew it. One 'mate' too many. Jim, Wullie and I went through the motions of turning out what pockets we had, that didn't already have holes in, confident we had no money, but not so confident that would do us any good at this point. Wasn't easy for Wullie as his hands had frozen in hamster mode and had to be prised away.

Egghead turned out his pockets and his satchel like Mary Poppins had taken up piracy. His satchel did contain an apple, an orange, corned beef pieces wrapped in foil (when was he going to share those?) and several school books still. Coin after coin was spilling out of each pocket wrapped in big sticky hankies, so they didn't jingle. He even had a pound note. A pound note!? Who carries around that kind of cash without security? I suppose technically we might have been the security, but he didn't tell us that. Fair's fair, though, we didn't tell him he was training to be our butler. As he produced his booty, he was beginning to bubble like a thirty-something watching a Bridget Jones movie.

'That's my dinner money for the week.' He bubbled.

There's the context if you needed it. This pound note could feed a boy for whole week. More than that...

'Nah it isnae. It's oor dinner money fur the week.'

..It would now feed three.

'You can huv these fur yur dinner.'

He was handed back the two sparrow's eggs, which he wrapped in his snotty hankie and put carefully in his pocket. The satchel was kept for the kestrel's egg and we all knew better not remind them it was not theirs.

I am pretty sure not all bigger boys grew up to be habitual, hardened criminals. I am sure most just developed into average law abiding bullies. Now that we had been robbed. Okay, technically Egghead was the only one 'robbed' of any possessions, but robbery is robbery. The experience is the same. You could sense a strange feeling of guilt in the bigger boys. Maybe they had taken it further then they intended. Whatever the reason they let us go with a nod and a wave.

'Fuck off then.'

You don't ask big boys twice, you just run and try not to look like you're running, apart from Egghead, who was sprinting ahead with tears and snotters now streamlining, like Amazonian tributaries, across his smooth noggin. By the time we caught up he was stuck at the bottom of a high wall, still running on the spot, in the hope that motion was going to get him over. It was a high wall. The kind of height you would normally walk miles to avoid climbing, but this time we had no choice. We had to 'puddy up' Egghead whose Daredevil skills were not yet developed.

As Wullie gave him one last heave, the eggs we forgot were still in his pocket, smashed in situ...erm...sorry...were released back into the wild. Our conservation project was complete. There were so many fluids oozing out of Egghead by this time, I don't even think he noticed the addition of a couple of unborn hedge sparrows.

Like any high wall it had to 'puddied up' one side and 'dreeped' on the other. Dreeping involved hanging on by your fingertips and lowering yourself as far as possible to minimise the drop. We knew this technique, of course we did. We had Commando skills. We'd seen it in the comics. But Egghead dropped like a sack of tatties off the top of the wall onto the right side. That's what spending your days reading Pride and Prejudice does. To this day I cannot read Humpty Dumpty without hearing the thud and crack of that fall. As we dreeped to his side like abseiling SAS types, Humpty, sorry Egghead, lay motionless for a few seconds. We used those few seconds constructively, to decide whether to run and leave him to the wolves or think about what we were going to tell his mum. Well, I was thinking anyway. Jim was kicking Egghead for signs of life and Wullie was doing his hamster hands.

'It's like this, Mrs McManus. Eggh...John.' Had to think of his real name.

'John made us go looking for eggs. He made us. Twisted our arms. He said if we didn't go he would batter us.'

'John made you?'

'Yes!'

'Our John was going to batter you?'

'Yes.'

'Our John made you do something you didn't want to do?'

'Yes?'

'Our Egghead?'

'Oh, you call him that too?'

Egghead stirred. Thank God for that. None of that was going to wash. We would have had to leave him behind. Save ourselves. Even in his dazed state, Egghead was suddenly up. Instinctively he took flight like an incontinent Bambi in a sniper's scope. He was running from his first big boy experience headlong into a potential hiding, but seemed keen to get there. Damage limitation I suppose. It still wasn't that dark though, but maybe dark enough for Mr McManus.

We couldn't resist stopping off, on our way home, outside his front door to hear his screams of explanation to his exploding father as he beat the living crap out of him. As I said, ahead of his time in parental technique. A new breed indeed. This might have been a good time to knock on the door and explain why he had wandered so far from home; how it was our fault; how we were training his son to be our butler; and how those eggs ended up in his pocket through no fault of his own. Or, in time honoured fashion, we could chap the door and run away to compound Egghead's problems, by agitating his father just a little bit more. Wullie took the decision out of our hands by doing precisely that.

He knocked. We ran!

Egghead would never agree to be the Daredevil's butler now.

CHAPTER 6

Where do the children play?

Maybe it was safer for a while to stick closer to home. After all, the street itself had much to offer as an adventure playground; pavements; the odd hedge; lampposts; dried white dog shit; stanks (drain covers); puddles, most of the time. Lots to offer! But it was safe. No gang could accost you in your own street. No big boys could come swaggering into your street in case the big boys in your street were even bigger. You only encountered such dangers when you ventured out.

The games we chose to play depended on numbers and maybe gender, gathering in the street. A group of boys would more often than not become a game of street football. In a street scenario this is a lot more random in terms of where the pitch and the goals were. The most conveniently placed lampposts were goalposts obviously and the pitch stretched as far as the street and beyond, if it got out of control, which it invariably did. If you had the misfortune of being in goal for one of these games, it could be weeks before you saw anyone as the game took off down the end of the street, way beyond any perceived pitch boundary, meandered off into side streets, down lanes and onto buses into the next town. Slight exaggeration there, but it felt like that. Not that many cars about back then, so no obstacles getting in the way or driving past.

If a large mixed crowd began to gather, bored out of their skulls, then it inevitably led to a game of 'Kick the Can'.

The supporting cast of usual suspects who would gather for these games included; Bear Lynch - real name John but we called him Bear perhaps because he was a boy mountain, or probably just a bit bigger than us; His brother Mikey Lynch, whose main life ambition was to own a Ford Anglia - I like to think he achieved that goal and now spends his Bank Holidays at Ford Anglia rallies; Tom McGladrigan, he didn't live in our street but was a cousin to the Lynch boys - He was a nice boy who had a large round head - picture Stewie from 'Family Guy', I always do; Wullie's younger brother Peter; Egghead, of course - lots of funny shaped heads going on.

These guys were the main players. I said a mixed crowd and failed to come up with any real girls names who joined us, though I think Wullie's sister Elizabeth is a likely contender. There were other possible players who lived up our own close but were never involved in our games. The Laird brothers from upstairs weren't joiners I don't think. Stuart was the older one and less memorable mainly because his younger brother Robert collected Bunty dolls. I am fairly certain his life path was set early doors.

Ruby Laird, their mother, had to fill in making our tea once, an occasion memorable for several things; 1.'Ruby, don't take your love to town' blasting out from inside as we were welcomed in. Ruby's love of the Kenny Roger's classic, written specially for her it seems, led her to blast this tune out at every opportunity; 2. My first taste of what I presumed to be nectar of the Gods. Not jam on her pieces, but Lemon Curd. I had never tasted anything so mind blowing in all my days and probably the reason I was once persuaded to drink from one of those plastic lemon juice things, shaped like an actual lemon, only to be told that someone had pissed in it. Almost ruined lemons for me forever until my first lemon meringue pie took me right back to Mrs Laird's kitchen.

As we munched our lemony treats we were led to Robert's bedroom so that he could enthuse over his collection of Bunty dolls, like Louie Spence on a panel show. We didn't know what to do. Maybe if they were like Action Man we could have played along or found some common ground, but Bunty dolls are not even real dolls, they are cut out of the back of the weekly Bunty magazine...for girls, with their cut our clothes and little tabs on so you can dress Bunty in the latest fashions. I know it was the sixties, but we weren't ready for that. We didn't even know what 'that' was. I was torn, though I will admit. My overriding feeling was, you really need to be sticking those main dolls to the back of a Kellogg's' Corn Flakes packet, Roberto, to give them the rigidity they need to hold the dress tabs. I wanted to offer this advice, but Robert's passion threw me. It was all too new to us. We couldn't join in. We just stared as Lemon Curd dribbled from our open mouths. We were carved out of cowboys and soldiers and guns and dirt and football. It's not better, it's just how we were then. Nurture or nature, it's safe to say Stuart and Robert in particular, were not the outdoorsy types. We needed people who weren't afraid to get their hands dirty for our games. Robert was too busy preparing for Paris Fashion Week.

That visit upstairs to Ruby Laird's ought to really have been memorable for the reason our own mum wasn't around to make our tea, rather than a bit of lemon curd and some paper dolls. If I think back she may well have been off giving birth to our youngest brother, Stephen, which was a valid enough reason not to make out tea, and you'd think it would be something we would remember or have been told. It was only one night though, so we thought nothing of it. Hardly broke our stride.

I'm sure others have their own derivative of 'Kick the Can' as it's basically hide and seek with added drama. The time honoured way of decided who was 'het', 'it', call it what you like, in any game was often the classic 'eeny meeny miny moe' technique. This, however, wasn't the most trust method as it was quite easy to work out who the poor sucker was likely to be depending on who you started with. It also fell out of favour for using the 'N' word later. As luck, rather than design, would have it, we had our own version that never included that anyway. Ours was more about babies shitting and wiping their bums - much more pleasant. It was the complete lack of mathematical complexity of 'eeny meeny miny moe' that we would argue over. Why it caught on and lasted so long I will never know?

Much more preferred was the 'One potato, two potato' technique. Each person has two potatoes (or hands), so it takes longer to work its way to the end. I'm not suggesting that the 'One potato, two potato' formula would have troubled Stephen Hawkin, it was just longer and we always forgot where we started by the end, so it seemed fairer.

These were all well and good for a traditional hide and seek game, but 'Kick the Can' needed something extra to make it work and this was inherent in the decision making. A can.

An in-depth knowledge of your neighbours eating and waste disposal habits would come in very handy at this point. Last one to find a can and bring it back to an agreed spot was 'het'. There was only one place to look - the middens. Large grey bins in the back court where everyone's rubbish went. No time to think, just leap into the bin and find a can. Any can. Covered in beans, dog food, whatever. No separation of food waste in those days. Oh no.

We tell people who will listen now that we used to play in the middens and that's why we never get colds now. Not strictly true. They were storage units for the stuff we needed, but we didn't 'play' in them. It wasn't like a clubhouse. We didn't get in there and sit around playing stud poker.

'What you got?'

'Three sixes, a five of clubs, two aces and the joker.'

'That's not even a hand.'

'I got a royal flush.'

'I'll raise you.'

'I'll see you.'

'I'll see you raising him, raise you a bit more and then raise myself.'

'You dirty rat!'

'Who you calling a dirty rat, you dirty rat?'

'You talkin' to me? You talkin' to me? You talkin' to me? Then who the hell else are you talkin' to? You talkin' to me? Well I'm the only one here. Who do you think you're talking to?'

'I was talking to the actual rat eating that rotting chicken leg.'

'Why are we in here?'

'What are we playing again?'

'Kick the Can.'

'Shit!'

'Can!!'

It wasn't just rat eat chicken, it was dog eat dog. Jim, Wullie and I were all in the same bin looking for the best can. My youth would work against me in that they were stronger, bigger and a little bit meaner, as they stood on my head to get out. I appeal to their better nature and our code of conduct.

'We're Daredevils, we should be helping each other, or at least starting a recycling scheme, because this is gross.'

'Can't stop. Write it in the journal for our next meeting.'

'If we start recycling now you could potentially kill off the game of 'Kick the Can' forever. People will begin to think it's morally and socially wrong to be kicking rubbish about the street, and then where would we be?'

Wulllie insightfully shouted as he ran off, without looking back.

Eventually my victorious hand appears out of the midden clutching a Heinz baked bean tin. The best kind. I scramble out, covered in bits of lettuce, despite no one ever eating lettuce, and rush to the can spot only to find I'm last. All that rummaging in shit for nothing. Everyone else just popped home quickly and asked their mums for one.

I'm 'het'! Brilliant. They all bugger off to hide with glee.

The second rule and the real jeopardy in the game is that as you move from the spot where the can is placed to search, you risk losing out more. Get too far from the spot and someone will leap out of hiding and run to kick the aforementioned can from here to Ballieston. If this happens too often you can be 'het' forever. You needed speed, cunning, guile and nerve. I had none of those things. I think I might still be 'het' now.

Hide and seek was easier as it didn't have the same nerve tangling tension, just a simple hide and, of course, seek. You could set off looking without the fear and trepidation of Kick the Can. To avoid us being lost forever we needed a signal to call us out of hiding. I say hiding, most of us were simply sat on a cold stair up a nearby close hoping not to chased out by an irate woman who lived there. I can't recall too many other ingenious hiding spots. The middens would have been great, but what if nobody came looking? How many were lost to the world by playing hide and seek on bin day? The tuneful cry of 'The Game's a Bogie' would call everyone out.

'The game's a bogie, the man's in the loaby. Come oot, come oot, wherever ye are.'

I don't know who the man is or why he was hanging about near the front door. I'm sure it's some Medieval reference to death or the Grim Reaper. The game's is up, the man is here to take you to the netherworld and all that nonsense. I don't know.

I do know you had better have a good excuse if you are ending the game and calling everyone out, especially someone with a good hiding spot that day. Invariably it was tea time. It was always tea time. Not the best excuse but always considered a valid one. You can't just be calling 'The Game's a Bogie' because you are rubbish at finding anyone. These people are coming out of hiding at you like Zombies on a mission for whatever it is Zombie are usually thirsting for.

'What did you dae that fur? Why is the Game a Bogie?'

'I have to go in fur ma tea.'

'I was up that close on a stair. It was ma best hiding spot ever.'

'I was under a hedge.'

'I was behind that lamppost.'

'I know I could see you fae here.'

'I had created a fifth dimension and was hiding through a time portal in the 21st Century, whilst earning a living as flying car salesman. It was ma best hiding spot ever.'

'Cannae be helped. I was shouted in fur ma tea.'

'Fair enough.'

'You shouldnae huv mentioned that portal, we'll aw be through that next time.'

'Where's Mikey Lynch?'

'I think he was hiding in a midden.'

Cue the clashing sound of an emptying midden and a bin lorry driving into the distance. Another one lost to a regular bin day.

Boredom was not a reason to terminate even the longest

search either. This wasn't boredom. These games were our 'Grand Theft Auto'; our 'Tetris'; our 'Call of Duty'- although that's more like Best Man Faller. These games were even our 'Pacman'; 'Space Invaders'; even our Pong. This was all we had. This was not boring.

This was three dimensional running about in a virtual reality world that existed only for us with no real connection to the rest of humanity, trying to find strange looking kids. This was 'Pokemon GO'.

A gentler pursuit was bools (marbles). Gentler physically, but a brutal introduction into the world of gambling really. Bools was played on a stank. Stick with me here. These stanks had holes and you roll the bools into the holes and somebody does something else and somebody wins the bools. The rules seemingly haven't stuck.

Everyone had their own collection of bools, some more beautiful than others. Hypnotising. Miniature crystal balls with coloured swirls trapped forever inside like small galaxies. Men in Black got that bit right. We fiddled with our bools, fiddled with each other's bools and made up games with no rules most of the time.

But one day a stranger showed up to play with a much larger and shinier collection including a prize deep blue bool. Wow, what beauty. This shit just got real! What Gods have formed this spherical wonder from the very heavens above? This bool was my particular 'precious'. What I should have noticed at that point, but didn't because of the 'precious', was what I just said, 'a much larger and shiner collection'. There was a reason for that. First, he probably knew the rules and secondly, he didn't get that collection because he was rubbish at bools. Do I risk it? Do I risk playing this Boris Spatsky of the bool stank for his 'precious' blue bool?

Of course I do. I've never seen a blue bool as beautiful as this. It's like a sapphire glinting in the bag. A small fragment of the deep blue ocean. I challenge him. I pull out my bools. He grabs his bools. Only he doesn't grab the deep blue bool. He produces a beat up, ordinary collection of murky, chipped glass baubles.

'What aboot the big blue bool?'

'What aboot it?'

'Are ye no using that?'

'Are ye kiddin? It's like a sapphire glinting in the bag. A small fragment o' the deep blue ocean. It's ma prize bool. Yur no havin' that.'

'I needs the blue bool. I needs it.'

'Yur no getting it. Play.'

I plays the game all the time watching the precious in the bag.

'I could bash his head on the pavements and take the precious. Yes! Yes! Bash his head. Bash, bash, bash. The precious is mine. All mine. Prec..i..ous!!'

Everyone is looking.

'Did I say all that out loud?'

Seems I did. He didn't need to be any good at bools now. He took my whole collection. I risked it all on blue and came out black and blue. Never gamble kids. That big shiny blue jewel that you say you can win, you can't win! Cos they don't bloody play with it. They just dangle it out promising you can play with it, and they keep dangling their blue bools in your face until you lose all hope and dignity. (too many bool euphemisms?)

I stuck to the world of five stones from that point. It's the common man's sport. All you need is five stones, surprisingly, and the back of your own hand. It's low risk and we would play it for hours..and hours..and hours. It was a game to play inside a close in the rain which is why we managed to hone our five stones skills to international levels. For every adventure and story set in the great outdoors in this book, there are a hundred hours stuck in a close out of the pissing rain playing five stones. This was our game. We were shit hot. We coulda been someone. We coulda been contenders. If we had the resources, the awareness of the bigger world and maybe a bit more bloody ambition, we could have put Jim up for the World Title. He had fighter's hands. Wullie wanted his shot at the title but he had a bad cold that day and besides his hamster hands would let him down and show a tendency to get nervous. Not to mention being covered in snotters now. So Jim was up. Wullie and I would be his corner men, rubbing moisturiser into Jim's hands to keep them supple. Yes, it sounds wrong now, but... but... Okay, it sounds wrong anyway, but try telling Jim it's wrong, when he still has the hands of twenty year old Ladyboy.

'Doodoodededoo   dededoodoodoo,   Doodoodededoo dededoodoodoo Badaba Badaba...'

Rocky theme? What?

Out of time and context, I get it. Thing is we only owned three records that I knew of, so it's either 'Mary's Boy Child' by Harry Belafonte; 'Tower of Strength' by Frankie Vaughan; or 'Walking Back to Happiness' by Helen Shapiro. Helen it is.

'Yay, yay, yay, yay ba dum be do. Yay, yay, yay, yay ba dum be do.'

Lets' get ready to ruuuuuumble!

'In the blue corner, the challenger. The lying, cheating, wouldn't put his big blue bool up for grabs, and is about to feel the wrath of "I'm gonnae set my big brother onto you." style justice - Blue Bool Man !'

Catchy.

'In the red corner, wearing what would've been a classy, red silk hooded robe if it hadn't been knitted by his granny and darned (not embroidered- we're not Victorians) with big DD symbol on the back - the one, the only, or he would be if there wasn't three of them...Daredevil!'

Ding!

We're off! Jim hits him with a big opening throw, catching all five stones on the back of his hand. Just a simple flip and catch and he will be off to great start.

He flips. He drops one. It slips.

Slips?

Bool Man is in. Bool man throws. He catches. He reverse throws, he catches. Game on now. He throws a stone in the air and picks up one stone...and two...and three...Easy. He knows it too. He barely even looked. He's smirking.

We waft towels near Jim's face, but not too near. If he loses his glasses we're all in trouble. Wullie sneezes, but manages to catch most of it on his sleeve, like a civilised person.

Bool man goes for four stones. Wullie sneezes again all over Bool Man.

He drops a stone.

'Ha! In your big fat face - literally.' I sportingly applaud his efforts.

Jim's in again.

Throw. Catch. Reverse throw. It's all going well. One stone, two stones. It slips out his grasp again. This never happens. What's going on?

Bool man is showboating.

We are wiping and rubbing Jim like demented Turkish

masseurs. Now is not the time to be coy. He has to be ready to take his chance. I grab his throwing hand. It slips out of mine. What?

Did you moisturise this morning?

I always moisturise. Right after I exfoliate.

He produces his exfoliating gloves. He has exfoliating gloves!! What is he thinking? Nobody moisturised and exfoliated. For God's sake, we thought smoking was good for your complexion then.

Jim is over moisturised. We have just moisturised an already moisturised and exfoliated 12 year old boy's skin. He has no purchase.

Bool man drops again on four. He bottled it.

This is our chance...to cheat. We quickly rub Wullie's jumper sleeve and a few additional fresh snotters, from Wullie streaming nose, all over Jim's throwing hand, and pitch him back into the ring.

After a slight gag, he throws. He catches. He reverse throws, he catches. The stones are sticking to him like fresh snotters on a sleeve. He picks up one stone..and two..and three...He's on a roll. He goes for four. This is the big one. Suddenly, his throwing stone sticks in his hand. The snotters are hardening. It's now or never. If his next try doesn't take off, the stone in his hand will have to be surgically removed from the only substance that ever gave the manufacturers of Superglue cause for serious concern - hardened child snotters.

We once flicked two snotters onto the ceiling of our bedroom in 1966 and they were still there in 1971 when we moved house. Now you could argue that is a black mark against our mother's cleaning regime, but we prefer to see it as the birth of Artex.

With superhuman effort and a loud crack, the throwing

stone breaks free of the bonding material and flies high into the air. It's all slow motion from this point. Jim is able to pick all four stones up one at a time and throw in a victory dance. The throwing stone lands back in his hand with a satisfying plop.

Bool man mouths,'Nooooooo!'.

Wullie sneezes again and the spray covers all of us like champagne at the end of Formula 1 race.

Victory! World Champions. The pinnacle of our five stones career.

Next day Jim went to hospital to have the snotters removed and we all had streaming colds for the next week, but what a moment.

Not every street day was quite this exciting. I spent many just ambling up and down picking leaves off hedges in gardens. Not country hedges where the sparrows were, just garden hedges, looking for tiny caterpillars in curled up leaves. As I said not every day was that exciting.

Sometimes I would put those leaves, with their passengers, in a puddle stream on the edges of the road and follow it till it dropped down a drain. As I said not every day was that exciting. That is not say there are not mutant butterflies living in the drains below our cities, just waiting to wreak revenge and take over the world. Once they have worked out how to live longer than a week. To be fair that's still longer than the aliens in War of the Worlds.

Why was dog shit white? There was a lot of white dog poo then and I was told it was dalmatian poo. Took me years and hundred of dalmatians, to find out that wasn't true. It was chalk added to dog food back then. They don't do it now. As I said not every day was that exciting.

The street had it's limitations. We were thrill seekers,

adventurers. It isn't that we never got bored then, of course we did. Out of our skulls. It's just that there was no easy way around that. No one had figured out ways to create games that meant we never had to leave our chairs to fulfill all of our wildest imaginations. We can be as sniffy as we like about all the Vitamin D deficient, obese, burger eating, spotty, square eyed kids of today, but who among us can honestly say that if those games were laid before us, that we would not have grasped them just as eagerly as kids do now. We had the misfortune to be born at the tail end of the industrial revolution and in that hiatus of time where the world was waiting for the communication age to begin. I thinks it's why everyone was shagging each other and talking about free love and all that nonsense. It's only because they had nothing else to do. And if you leave mankind long enough with nothing else to do, he will always think about sex. God should have given Adam and Eve jobs to do.

The communication age would come. Action man was a clear indicator of that. A toy whose limbs could move and you could pretend was a real person? Come on! A ba' hair's width from artificial intelligence and robots taking over. But until that day we had to get out there and make our own fun.

The street wouldn't hold us for long.

CHAPTER 7

The potato famine

The more well known, and popular, potato famine of course took place from 1845- 1952 in Ireland, which doesn't really fall into the timeline of this particular tale, though the connection is stronger than you might think. When I say 'popular' of course it wasn't all that popular at the time, as millions died and millions more had to leave their homeland. Many of them moved to the west coast of Scotland where we have discovered our direct descendency to those very same Irish folk who fled the famine. See what a bit of research can throw up? The family connection wasn't my research of course, but brother Jims' and beyond that I Googled it. I also discovered in my extensive months of research that there have been other potato famines, but they aren't the ones I want to delve into right now. The one I feel I have to put into black and white is the one I'm sure we caused.

Now before you start thinking that the Daredevils went 'rogue' and began using their superpowers to destroy the world, or the potatoes of the world at least, that wasn't it. Though to be fair that would make a great film sequel as long as everything turned out all right in the end.

'Oh my gosh! What's happening?'

'Look, it's the Daredevils in black jump suits destroying all of our potatoes.'

'Why would they do that?'

'Why potatoes?'

'Have they gone mad?'

'They've gone rogue!'

'Look at them they are really cutting up all those potatoes.'

'I can't look!'

'What hope is there for the world if the Daredevils have taken to destroyi...Oh no wait..Look..They're making chips.'

Now if only we had thought of such a practical solution to our own potato dilemma. We were happily wandering through the longy trying to assess if it was ready for burning again, when we literally stumbled across lots of bags of potatoes. Just lying around in the long grass near the derelict building that were sure was a Medieval World War 2 bunker, strategically positioned overlooking the canal. What do you do when you come across lots of bags of potatoes? Well the chip option is a good one. Cook something from arguably the most versatile vegetable in the universe. Actually I am not even sure there is an argument. Lettuce - very limited, as is a cabbage. Onion. A good vegetable, don't get me wrong but when have you ever done anything other than cut up an onion to put it in something? Mushroom, pepper, chilli and broccoli. All fine, but bit part players. And don't even get me started on tomatoes. The only vegetable that runs the potato anywhere near close, and it's supposed to be a bloody fruit! It isn't of course. We all know that. The tomato knows that, and so do all the other fruits.

For some reason that can't be explained or understood in this age of celebrity chefs, eating the potatoes wasn't high on our list. This was a time when, for us, potatoes meant a boring Monday meal. Tatties and mince. Always tatties and mince. Other days maybe a few chips with fish fingers (Friday obviously) or the odd potato croquet with spam. We weren't given to sudden flights of fancy with dauphinoise potatoes or pomme fondant. We ate what we were given, (mostly) and what we were given did not require much preparation beyond peeling, frying or boiling. I am aware now that a sophisticated developing world did exist outside of ours back then. A world where proper chefs were cooking gourmet meals for discerning clientele in fancy restaurants. Where potatoes took on a whole new life. A life of style and glamour. Those big time potatoes knew how to sauté down a red carpet.

You would think that even though there were too many potatoes for us to eat, about six bags I recollect, (Now you and I both know, by now, that I made that up, but there were a few) that we would see the potential in other people eating them. But it never crossed our minds to sell them on, which also shows an acute lack of business acumen, that stays with me to this very day, because we could have sold the bloomin' potatoes and made a fortune. Well, a relative fortune. Enough to not have to eat ha'penny caramels for a month or so. A sweetie fortune.

So what did we do with this delicious booty? What masterful plan the socially conscious dynamic trio the Daredevils dream up to help make the world a better place?

We thought it would be a good idea to lay them out on the canal road and see if a truck went by and skidded on the potatoes and into the canal.

No really that was the plan. Really!!

There was no one to tell us this wasn't a good plan. It wasn't a good plan, but you never know till you try. We tried things out and got most things wrong. If things went so wrong that parents found out then you knew you gone too far. Kids didn't get grounded in those days. We got the living crap beaten out of us, in a loving way, learned our lesson and went about our business again with our arses stinging. So you knew not to make the same mistake twice. That didn't discourage us from inventing new mistakes. Most of our plans would go wrong in some way, but never so badly that parents ever found out. That was the skill. You had to push the envelope so far without it being addressed to mum and dad. I think that even the worst plans we had were, in their own perverse way, highly successful in that regard.

It was time to tip some coal lorries into a canal. In a sweet and innocent way of course. Any ensuing or potential tragedy was not our fault. How could it be?

It shouldn't even need mentioning that this was in the days before health and safety existed. There was no triple layer of Arnco at the side of this canal or foot thick concrete barrier to prevent potential accidents. This was a road...beside a canal. No one saw any real reason to add anything else.

'There you are, Paddy, we've finished the road.'

'Well done, Mick. (I know, I know) And sure enough we've just finished the canal right there beside it.'

'Now isn't that a pretty site, sure enough?'

'Indeed it is Mick. Indeed it is.'

'Do you think it needs any finishing touches?'

'Like what, Mick?'

'I don't know really. Maybe a little barrier of some kind.'

'For what purpose Mick?'

'Maybe it'll be safer.'

'Safer? Safer than what? We've built the canal.'

'Yes and very nice it is too, Paddy.'

'And you've built the road right there beside the canal. Well done for that, Mick. Now if you had built the road on top of the canal I can see your point, Mick. But in accordance with the actual plans, you have built the road right beside the canal. Parallel you might say.'

'That I have, Paddy.'

'Now if all the right vehicles stick to the right surface, there shouldn't be a safety issue of any kind, Mick. As long as no arsehole comes along and puts a load of slippery potatoes on the road, everything will be fine.'

Sooo...as I said, we thought it would be a good idea to lay them out on the canal road and see if a truck went by and skidded on the potatoes and then headlong into the canal. We didn't really have much idea how slippy an uncooked raw potato actually is. Now if it was mash I could see the reasoning in our thinking.

But of course if it was mash, then we would have already got round the whole 'What are we going to do with these potatoes?' thing. But I think our mothers would have had something to say about us humping six bags of potatoes into the house to peel and mash them before carefully gathering up the mashed concoction into various receptacles to transport them back to the canal road and spread them carefully over the newly laid Tarmac surface. As I have hinted at before, we could barely get into the house to grab a drink of water back then. We all drank water back then, and in those days it came out of a tap. Even so you had to sneak back into the house like a Ninja to get a drink at all. Mother had ears like a bat. Good hearing I mean not actual bat like ears.

'Who's that?'

'It's me. I've just come into to get a drink of...'

'Get out to play...'

'But I need a...'

'Out to play!'

'But I...'

'Out!'

No idea what mother was up to, but whatever it was we never got the chance to find out. So the idea of getting past her with six (we're sticking with six now, having established that) bags of old potatoes. It would have taken an operation on the scale of the tunnel digging in 'The Great Escape'. We would have been sneaking potato slices into the house, in our turn-ups, after dark for weeks.

The 'after dark' bit has nothing to do with the cover of darkness, that is well used in all the best escape movies, it was actually the only time we were allowed back into the house.

We were, however, no more expert in safe driving techniques than we were in cooking, so we really had no idea how a ten ton truck might react as it drove over potatoes. For all we knew it could have aquaplaned right into the canal. I have no idea if your average truck actually weighs ten ton. I suppose it depends on the load, but it sounds pretty heavy and it's a good round figure.

But not one of our best decisions as a group of aspiring superheros. The kind of decision in life that could have turned us to the dark side without even knowing there was a dark side. It hadn't been invented yet..like Lycra. This wasn't the only stupid or life threatening decision we would make by any means, though. Oh no, we had loads more up our sleeves. Lots of boundaries to push. Winds to sail close to. Maybe if we had bitten the bullet and made costumes, we might have thought some of these things through a bit more. Made ourselves a bit more visible. Put our heads above the parapet, so to speak I mean when Spidey goes a bit mental everyone know about it. It's front page news in the Daily Bugle.

'Look it's Spiderman!'

'What is he doing with those potatoes?'

'I have no idea.'

'Is he laying them out on that road?'

'Has he gone mad?'

'Does he know we can see its him in that garish Lycra outfit?'

'What's Lycra?'

'Sorry woolen.'

'He could cause an accident.'

'Oh my God, here comes a ten ton truck.'

'It going to drive right over them and crash right into that unprotected canal.'

'I can't bear to look.'

'Call J. Jonah Jameson.'

He was messing about! He is only human after all, even though his molecular structure was altered when he was bitten by the radioactive spider. He was out playing in his Spiderman outfit and he came across some potatoes and made a bad decision. If it can happen to him, it can happen to a Daredevil... or two...or three.

We weren't bitten by radioactive spiders but I was stung by a bee once. At least I think I was stung. It might have just been a small insect bite but as my own molecular structure, for that moment, had been altered to that of a six year old girl who had been mauled by a large bear, I had to stick with the story that I had been stung. I have never been stung.

Fully immersed in our potato scheme, threats like big boys couldn't have been further from our minds. We had white boards, models, spreadsheets spread all over the longy, trying to work out the likely outcome of ten ton truck meets King Edward. It was like Scrapheap Challenge without the scrap. It may be because we had raised our heads above that parapet with our potato plan, that we got noticed again. Out of the long grass came the three big boys. Not looking quite so scary as before. Slightly smaller against the long grass, or had we had a bit of a growth spurt? Either way we knew them this time and could jump right in with the 'mate' thing right away. Trouble is, this time something cast a shadow over them. This isn't a metaphor. There was a huge shadow that loomed behind them. As they got closer the shadow turned into a shape against the sky. We squinted into the direct sunlight and you're not supposed to do that. Luckily before our retinas were scorched, the Sun was blocked out as the shape loomed ever closer right behind the big boys. Not so lucky as it turned out actually. This wasn't an eclipse. Which was just as well as I don't think we knew what an eclipse was, and I am convinced we would have thought the world was ending. Nobody mentioned eclipses at school. The world wasn't ending, but as the shape became clear and now loomed over us, we were sort of wishing it would.

They had brought a Big Girl. A very big girl. She was scarier, bigger and much more butch than they were, and she did all the talking. Dominant women still scare me to this day.

'What you doing?' She boomed.

It was a boom. She definitely boomed.

'Nothing.'

'Aye ye ur.'

Meaning, of course, I am aware you are doing something, you better come clean or I am going to tear you a new one. With lesser mortals this could have gone on for some time. With her, we gave in.

'We just found these potatoes.'

That sounded much more butch in my head.

'Ye found tatties?'

It was a booming Fee Fi Fo Fum moment.

Wullie spilled the whole plot, in the hope it would make us look good.

'We're putting them on the canal road to see if any coal lorries slip on them.'

'Yur whit?'

'Ye'll kill somebody.'

'No, we'll no.'

'Aye ye wull.'

'We'll no.'

'Ye might.'

'It's just for a laugh.' Wullie explained.

'Pick them up.' She growled.

Great, now the big girl and her big boy sidekicks were sounding like the responsible ones. Which of course they probably were, but that isn't the point. We couldn't just back down and give in to a girl. Even one as huge and butch as this one.

For the record, Women's lib and all that had also not reached our street. We didn't really know what a bra was and had never seen one except the odd construction of our mothers that was sometimes left lying about. They weren't feminine or titillating objects for us. You couldn't burn one of those, you would set the house on fire. It wasn't an equality issue. We were obviously no equals to this monster. But she was still...a girl.

This girl wasn't wearing a bra anyway and if her butch mannerisms were any indication of her life's path...still doesn't. Girls didn't go for wearing such things at the age of ten as they do now. Nowadays ten year olds wear make up, earrings, a tattoo, a fake tan and a mini skirt to look 'sexy'. This girl was dirty though. No, I mean actually dirty. Covered in dirt. Caked in it. Or was it hair? She was still backlit by the Sun mostly so, hard to tell.

We looked to our 'mates' for support and they were obviously just as scared of her as we were. We had been wondering why they brought her, but now it was clear that she probably brought them.

'Take thum aff the road, eejits!'

She meant business. She had picked up, and was now brandishing with intent, an engineered half brick from the Medieval ruin. A half brick, by the way, that she could comfortably get her hand around. That is one big hand. Half bricks are hard to hold in small hands, but she wielded this half brick in her mutant paw like a mitten. Who was this evil genius?

We never did know her name. She had to be the big sister of one of the big boys. I stopped calling them Deatheaters now as they didn't look anywhere near as scary as what they brought with them this time.

Big Bertha!

We made up that name for her much later and from a safe distance. Why would she be hanging about with these boys? None of us had the skills to acquire a girlfriend, so it couldn't have been that.

Our generation were the result of the tail end of the baby boomer generation. Just as well our parents were at it like rabbits. We would never have achieved that boom. We could barely look at girls till the age of thirty never mind all that... sexy stuff. We eventually had babies without a bloody clue what we were doing. Our parents had all the fun. Post War (not the fun bit) they had to get out there (or in there) and keep the species going. It was expected. It was their job. They probably had pamphlets explaining this. We were left, because of the swinging sixties thing, to our own devices. Everyone assumed we knew what to do and forgot we were nine years old during the summer of love. By the time we got to whatever the right age was, we had no idea. No idea of the consequences. Well, we knew what they were once the consequences were laid before us in a second-hand pram (up-cycled as we call it now). By the age of seventeen, we knew we could get a girl pregnant. She knew we could get her pregnant. Our parents knew we could get pregnant. But there was one insurmountable barrier to the whole thing.

We were Catholic.

So between our parents not wanting to talk about it, but at the same time pressurising us into early loveless marriages if it happened; us not really bringing it up and just hoping for good timing and the best, babies boomed through sheer ignorance. 'Girlfriend' was not a term or a species we had yet encountered.

Big Bertha wasn't anybody's girlfriend.

Eejits? Interesting.

Nothing too sweary. Of Gypsy stock, possibly, yet still maintaining a ladylike quality under that manly front. It's hard to know where you stand. If it wasn't for the half brick, we might not have taken her all that seriously. I would have gone with 'wankers' or 'little shits' or something more aggressive sounding to make my point. She didn't need it. She knew we were intimidated enough by the fact she was a girl-ish. Why did we quiver and quake so much? We had big sisters. They weren't scary at all. Girls usually use the fact that they are girls, to assume power over boys. Big Bertha was an expert.

Some things never change I suppose. The promise of a flash of knicker would probably keep most boys strung along for weeks doing a girl's bidding. That was it! This was no sister. This was a twelve year old slut! She had promised them a flash of knicker or even a look at her...you know..her...you know...I'm not saying it...You know! Boy did she have power.

These boys weren't even producing testosterone yet and she had them wrapped round her little...you know. I can't help but imagine their disappointment when the moment of truth finally came.

'Show us then.'

'Maybe.'

'Show us!'

'Don't want to.'

'Aye you do.'

'I'm a lady.'

'Fuck off are you a lady. Show us yur knickers.'

'I'm no wearing any.'

One big boy faints at this point. There are only two left standing.

'Show us then.'

There is the long game of flash and swirl as he plays them like a matador with a bull. Then she finally gives them the flash and they are slain.

'She's goat a willie!'

'She's a bloke!'

'It's bigger than oors.'

'Wouldnae be hard, she's twelve!'

I'm speculating of course, because for now they are strung along, unaware of their possible fate. Like picking up a Ladyboy in Bangkok..apparently.

'Yeh, pick them up, eejits.'

The Big Boys backed her up now, with all the bravado of knowing which side your bread was buttered. Eejits didn't work for them in the same way. You could tell they would be more comfortable with 'wankers', but given the sway BB had over them, it wasn't their call.

Half brick or no half brick, we had neither the social skills, the balls...nor any real case to argue. She was like an assassin. You never doubt their intent. Threats are never idle. There were three of us. Fully initiated Daredevils, yet we daren't challenge her.

Wullie's hamster hands slowly raised into position. No point in looking to him now. He's a goner. Jim would pummel anyone in his way, but she was a girl, more or less. Only she knew how much, for now. In my head I was thinking I could reason with her.

'Now, Bertha I appreciate you think this show of aggression is a way of asserting authority over juniors and I am sure in the call centre office or Bangkok strip club where you will eventually carve out a career, that it will prove a useful tool, as will a...you know. But you're really compensating for some social, or character deficiency and it's that root cause that you should be channeling your aggression towards, not three hapless - albeit Daredevilly hapless - young boys just trying to have a bit of fun with some potatoes.'

She would break down and agree. Tell me she has a willie, show me it, and we would all move on, into therapy. But that stayed in my head, till now. Not the best approach - thinking of something clever to say forty years after the fact. The fact is, at this point, I had nothing!

We obligingly made our way down the slope to the road to remove the potatoes. Bertha decided it would be a great game to throw other potatoes at us whilst we did this. That was scary. Having stuff thrown at you, is scary. It is really hard to look butch, in any way as you scream like a girl trying to avoid a flying potato. At least she didn't go with the half brick. Small mercies, though when a King Edward bounces square off your noggin.

As we reached the bottom of the slope and almost out of Bertha's Herculean range, everything suddenly transformed into slow motion.

A fully laden coal lorry was coming!

What to do? As Daredevils, and in superhero mode, there were oh so many ways to save the day. We would have to think fast and use all of our super powers.

If we were Spiderman, (or men) despite being in an area of long grass and little other vegetation, a convenient tree would appear so that we could shoot our web and swing across to the oncoming truck; leaping into the drivers seat to take control; realise he was a better driver then we were anyway and then swing out again, shooting our web across the road catching the truck like a fly, just in the nick of time.

As Superman we would have no issues other than his identity problem. Despite the nearest phone box being about a mile away, at the train station, we could easily get there in time, after making a lame excuse to leave, and speed back again lifting the lorry over the potatoes to safety.

As Batman it is getting a little trickier. If you are hanging around the long grass as Bruce Wayne then you'll be useless. It's a long way back to the Batcave and all that's in there is a dead Scottie dog anyway. Aquaman is only any use once the lorry is in the drink.

So it's down to us and despite being Daredevils in our heads, we were in fact mere mortals when the chips were down. (chips..see what I did there?) Or maybe we were trying to protect our alter egos. You can't just whip off your ripped denims and reveal your powers to all and sundry. Once your real identity is known to the likes of Big Bertha, who was clearly an evil genius, your loved ones would never be safe again. Sometimes you have to meet these situations head on in mortal form.

As mortals, we still had some heroic options. The day was not yet lost and this lorry is moving in very slow motion.

Option 1: Jump out in front of the oncoming ten ton truck to stop it.

Option 2: Wave your arms about and attempt to point to the potatoes and express the danger of the situation in an added expression of fear.

Option 3: Actually lay down in the road to and hope the driver sees you in time.

Option 4: Wait and see what happens.

We went with option 4. We waited. Slowly ducking down into the long grass just in case.

The truck passed.

Nothing happened.

Ten ton trucks seemingly just squash potatoes if they get in their way. Who knew? Unless he was some kind of Evel Knievel stunt driver. We knew. Of course we knew. How could you not know that a potato is no match for a ten ton truck? A ten ton truck that has now come to a halt, just passed the potatoes with a burly driver getting out of the cab.

He's seen us.

'Oi! You little shits.'

Now he's talking our language. Now we knew where we stood. In the shit!

'Where did you get all these potatoes?'

That's his only concern? Where? Not 'It must have taken you ages to cut up all these potatoes and lay them out on the road'. No appreciation of the sheer effort and determination. We wanted to explain our creative thinking, but as it involved a potential near death experience for him...this wasn't the time.

Big Bertha and her boys helped us out and covered their arses.

'It wisnae us! It wis them!'

As they disappeared into the long grass and beyond, one last mighty potato that soared way over our heads and landed at Evel Knievel's feet. It had to be Bertha, she was the only one with that power. We stood our ground for a bit looking at each other. Nothing happened so technically, we weren't in any real trouble. Were we?

'I said. Where did you get all these potatoes? Did you nick them?'

Ah! He thinks we stole them. How could we steal six bags of potatoes? What kind of getaway driver would we need for such a heist? One like him probably.

'Okay here's the plan boys. We pick up the loot here...Carry it to here and dump it in the long grass.'

'Carry it?'

'Carry it.'

'It's heavier than six bags of potatoes, boss.'

'It's gold bullion.'

'It's still feels like six bags of potatoes. We need a driver.'

'Know anyone?'

'I've got a mate who drives ten ton coal lorries.'

'Any good?'

'Good? He's practically Evel Knievel. I've seen him drive over all sorts of shit.'

'Buses?'

'No, not buses.'

'Cars?'

'People?'

'Potatoes. He drives over potatoes.'

'Anybody can drive over potatoes. They're just potatoes.'

'They weren't cooked.'

Evel took one step towards us and we ran. We didn't just run. We pretended we were the Flash. He would never catch us if we did that. We ran with all legs and arms pumping at high speed. More legs than arms when you're being the Flash. So fast we were over-rotating as our legs tried to break the sound barrier. As we ran we felt the need to tell each other we were the Flash, in case anyone was in any doubt.

'Come'n make it, I'm the Flash.'

'So am I.'

'You're no fast enough I'm the Flash. Look.'

Jim sped out in front leaving Wullie and I behind. Wullie was trying to be the Flash whilst still doing his hamster hands thing, You can't do that. You need balance. It was a trick he would have to sort out later in life. We would soon catch up with Jim, though as she over-rotated and fell over.

Needless to say, in the end, we got away. Evel Knievel was no match for the Flash. I don't think he even tried. It was enough for him that we ran and, in his eyes, learned our lesson. We never did find out where the potatoes came from or which gang had carried out that audacious heist. Interestingly, the very next day you couldn't buy a potato at Galbraiths for love nor money.

One thing had changed though. The big boys weren't so big anymore. We had caught them up a bit and we had bonded over one thing. It was unspoken, but we knew it...and they knew it...

And they knew we knew it...And we knew they knew we knew it...And they knew we knew they knew we knew it. The next time we met them they would all know it. But no one would say a word about it.

We were all scared of a girl. If Big Bertha could be described as such. What we needed to do is get into a room, get in touch with our feelings, and have a good cry over how scared we felt. But that wasn't the done thing.

The done thing...was to prove you weren't.

CHAPTER 8

Running with the cows

It's a funny thing, courage. Are you born with it? Can you learn it? How do you even know you possess it? Maybe it's something in the water. Surely fear of Big Bertha is not lack of any real courage, but the natural fear of being hit with a half brick. Which is basic survival instinct, is it not? Neanderthals feared the larger Homosapiens and many people believe their extinction was due to conflict with, and displacement by, the rival, more dominant species. Though I really don't understand what they were afraid of. Having encountered Big Bertha, I am pretty sure that, if the boffins had only checked, they would have discovered that Neanderthals went from strength to strength and survived at least till the 'swinging sixties' in the east end of Glasgow.

So, discovering whether you have any in-built courage or bravery is down to life's experience testing you at the right time, in the right way. Bravery is a choice. Bravery is not about being ill. Given the choice we would not be ill. People who are ill have no choice. Bravery is how you deal with it. You can be scared and brave at the same time. The two are not mutually exclusive.

We were scared of BB. Scared of being maimed. Scared of flying missiles launched with Tessa Sanderson like force. Yes I choose Tessa over the more popular and modern Jessica Ennis Hill, even though Jessica may now hold new records for shot putt etc...I haven't checked. It doesn't matter. Part of the fear is the Neanderthalesque expression on the face of the thrower. Jessica looks too nice. She looks like she would apologise if it hit you. Tessa was aiming for you.

Life's experience tested many us times. You don't usually know you're being tested until it's too late and you're perched on the edge of a bath screaming like two year olds.

It wasn't our choice to share a bath. Everybody did it then. I have yet to meet someone from the sixties who bathed alone. I am not talking here about the swinging sixties of sexual liberation where sharing a bath was a cool and groovy exercise in foreplay, (a new thing back then) or a way of throwing off the oppressive shackles of the past. That kind of bath sharing would have looked shocking to us back then. Terrifying even. The problem is TV could at times catch us all out. There were some racy Play for Today programmes and when they were sprung on a family with no warning, suddenly you were trapped in front of it. There it is happening on screen. Two people in a bath, with no bubbles. The first time you have had a good picture, with no big black line, in months and WHAM! Naked bodies in murky bath. You couldn't move. You couldn't twitch. You couldn't even blink. TV producers knew this. They knew you had to actually get out of your chair to change the channel, so they had you. Trapped. Watching. Viewing figures went through the roof. Yes there was a watershed, but I don't go straight to bed after Blue Peter anymore.

Trouble is your parents also couldn't move. Couldn't twitch. Couldn't even blink. One tiny sign of movement would alert you to the fact that they could see it. And if you knew they could see it, maybe you thought they liked it. And if they knew you could see it, maybe they thought you understood it. There was only one solution and it had to happen quickly.

'Right!...Bed!...Now!'

There couldn't be the usual discussion normally employed to delay bedtime.

'Aw, but daaaaad I'm watching that.'

'Bed.'

'I want to see what happens now that the couple are naked and touching each others' bits in the bath.'

'Nothing happens.'

'Are you sure? Look at his face.'

'It's finishing in a minute.'

'I don't think so, dad. He's only just managed to fondle the first tit. He has a long way to go now and given they are both naked in a bath, she isn't really going to stop him. Oh what's that in the water?'

'BED!!!'

No, none of this. This was serious. Reaction had to be instant and it still had to look as if you hadn't see what you had seen. You moved swiftly, but threw in a quick yawn on the way as if you were planning for bed anyway. Everyone was happy with that. There were no videos, DVDs or play it again to worry about. It happened. It was dealt with. Move on. Nothing to see.

Real baths were shared for economical reasons. And dirty water for the same reasons. We didn't mind, Jim and I. We had some great games of soldiers in the bath. It was always important to take your favourite soldiers in there with you. The German ones who looked like they were crawling on the ground were best because you could imagine they were swimming. Things were going well. Soldiers were diving from a great height into the murky depths performing triple pike loops on the way...and then it happened. The bravery test! Nobody knows how.

Well, biologically I have a fair idea. I do have a Higher in Biology. Grade C that took me two years to achieve. Suddenly, there was something in the water. You can try to imagine the 'Jaws' music, in your head, if you like, but this was so long before that. It was more Hitchcock's 'Physco'. I can't remember warning Jim that something was amiss. To be honest, as I remember, it was a bit of a shock to us both. Nonetheless there it was...floating dangerously upstream towards Jim. It's only when you see the gravitational pull of the moon in all its wave forming glory that you full appreciate it, as it was being pulled towards Jim's side of the bath. There was nothing either of us could do except the bravest thing we could think of. We leapt out of the bath and perched on the sides screaming and pointing. I don't quite recall how mother scooped the 'enemy sub' out of the bath that day, but more worryingly, I don't remember getting out afterwards.

I hold my hands up now to being the culprit and if I am holding myself to account for that, I would like another incident in the classroom one day, where all control was lost, to be taken into consideration your honour. I say all control was lost. It wasn't really. What was lost was the inability, through painful shyness, to actually ask the teacher if I could 'leave the room.' That made for a very lonely and painful walk home that day. A walk I will never forget. Have you ever really pooped your pants? I mean properly filled them? And then tried to walk for miles as if you hadn't a care in the world?

What I don't remember is what happened to those pants. I either threw them out, which I can't believe was possible, as it was mother who bought the pants in those days, so she had them all counted. Or I just put them in the wash thinking she wouldn't notice. She never mentioned it.

Obviously we failed to show any real courage on that occasion, but the bath wasn't a true test of courage, it was more a test of how far we were prepared to go to share water and save electricity, because I am pretty sure our younger brothers went in after us.

I think cows tested our courage to our limits. But we tested them too. Maybe that was the point of the exercise. We knew it. The cows definitely knew it.

To one side of our wasteland was a farmer's field. It ran all down one side. You can see it on the 'Narnia' map. Check the entrances and exits to that field, it will come in handy later, for reference.

Again, I can't help but think that nowadays the idea of living so close to nature and fields, would be pure bliss for parents and children alike. There would be an established touchy, feely, strokey animal farm, where annoying kids would get to punch pigs in the face when mummy wasn't looking. The farm would be run by TV personalities and would make it's own cheese and ice cream. Yummy Mummys would gather to drink skinny cappuccinos, sat on replica milk churns, whilst their kids played in an 'adventure playground' with non stick slides and rubber tyre swings and feather pillows on the ground, to avoid terminal grazing of the knee. Petting zoos, that's what they call them.

Petting? Zoos? Where to start with all that? You don't get to pet animals in zoos. They are in zoos because they will break your arm, like a swan, if you get anywhere near them, or worst case scenario, eat you. The kind of animals in petting zoos now were, in those days, kept in fields. Our cows were in a field. They weren't usually in there and I still don't fully understand the whole field rotation thing. There was never anything but grass in there anyway. This was our normal field for collecting bees. Like Darwin remember? Take a jar, put some bee flowers in it, which I have since learned are dandelions...before they get all 'dandy'. I would like to say the flowers were in there to make them feel at home, once trapped in a boiling hot glass dome with no means of escape, but the truth is that the flowers were there to attract them to their doom. Holes were pierced in the jar lid. Again not really for their breathing convenience, more to prolong their agony, so that we could look at them for longer. It was a cruel sport, but then country sports often are when viewed from a certain perspective.

We had a problem this particular day other than the cows pooing all over the bees. This day we had to take our little brother, Paul along with us. He was a cute enough kid with a fairly flattish head that we never at any point felt the need to mention to him. Never once did we compare his head shape to that of a standard wardrobe. That would have been cruel and uncalled for, so let's say that never happened. Let's say we never noticed. He was only six, so to be calling him those kind of names at that age would be mean. Unless of course everybody saw it as a funny or cool nickname, like my Dumbo one. 'Wardrobe Head' was like his rapper name. Cool and streetwise. Like 'Pud' for instance. Pud was our 'cool rapper name' for the even younger and more sensitive brother, Stephen. He had a rounder head and again cute as a button, so it fitted. It was affectionate. He wasn't so keen, but at least he gets to have the last laugh now with that moniker. Paul just had to grow his hair longer.

So as I said, we had a problem. Paul's lack of aerodynamics would also prove to be an issue before the day was out.

I say we had to take him, but I think mother meant take care of him. She should have been more specific. Jim, Wullie, me and a young 'un tagging along. A few years younger and probably not of an age that our mother should have left him in our charge. Not if she knew half of what we got up to. But mothers never do, and what she didn't know wasn't going to kill her. The same can't really be said for little Paul though.

Today, we were the big boys, even me. And with no other

big boys around or big girls for that matter, we could set our own bar. I don't know why cows look an easy target. Maybe it's because, side on, they are exactly that...a big, easy target. Maybe it's because they don't seem to mind what goes on around them. Or so we thought back then. Mild cows. Passive cows. Cows in the sixties must have been on different kind of grass from cows today. They had a good reputation then. Nobody says cows are mild mannered now. Oh no. I have testimonials.

'Don't go in field with cows they will crush you to death... To death!'

'Cows look evil. They have shifty eyes.'

'A cow will pick you up and maul you like a rag doll.'

Cows are the new swans! Nobody thought that about cows then. Maybe some farmers died at their hands, but they kept that quiet and we didn't have Countryfile. Responsible for more deaths worldwide now than the hippo. Someone should check that stat, but regardless, they do a have different reputation now. Maybe they sussed how many of them we eat now, and are fighting back a bit. Other than the odd Wimpy nobody was really eating burgers over here in the sixties. Nowadays most cow career paths would lead towards being a burger, but then the only meat we ever had was mince, and that is me stretching our world beyond its borders to the big city. In our world we had never seen a burger. A sausage, yes, but that's pigs. Spam. Pigs again, mostly. Steak was out of the question except for Desperate Dan who ate a lot of cow pies. Even with that kind of blatant product placement, we still never ate any beef in our house outside of mince and tatties. So it is probable that the average cow had not yet considered man a natural predator, and it is the fact that they have seen through our supposed kindness, that makes them a bit edgy now.

Or...it might have been us who set them off on that road.

Whose idea it was to throw stones at the cows? Nobody has ever admitted blame in that respect. We were all trying to be big boys to impress our little brother and they were sort of in the way of the bees we were out to collect We were sure that you could throw a stone at a cow without hurting it. It's a big thing a cow. A stone is a little thing. So it is effectively throwing stones at a moving wall. For all the guilt we feel now about throwing stones at cows, I can't help but thinking that until that point, in that field, on that day, all cows were easy going and minded their own business. We may have set them off thinking otherwise. Stories may have been passed on from cow to cow, from field to field, that man, and in particular three and a half small men, were not to be trusted. Man was mean. Man was aggressive without provocation.

'If you see a man in a field, break his arm before he uses it to throw something at you.'

You have to remember we didn't have Playstations!

I know we complain about our fat kids, and yes, they will all die an early obese death or lose their toes through diabetes later in life, but the alternative is equally horrific...for the cows. So stay indoors kids, eat burgers, steal cars, rape Ho's and get fat. Given the opportunity we would have done the same. We would have thrown stones at virtual cows and people would have complained on black and white TV programmes. But no actual cows would have been harmed and we wouldn't have considered the option of finding actual cows to stone. The game is the thing. Real or actual is not the point.

However the point is, virtual reality did not exist. We only had actual reality. So the game was simple. Try to hit a cow with a stone. There was no points system, I mean, we weren't sickos! Stupid, not sick. I don't really think little Paul was as impressed by our grown up game as we had hoped. There is no way to remember for him or us. Mainly because that was not the memorable bit of the day. I said there was no points system, but this didn't mean there was no challenge. The big cows have baby cows. Calves they call them. We call them. They don't call them anything. Anyway, smaller cow, bigger challenge. I don't want to paint a more gruesome picture as I don't want to alienate animal lovers completely from the book buying demographic. You see for yourself where this is going.

Glad you do. We didn't. What happened next has now been well documented by many a rambler, but we had never seen such a thing. The cows got a bit upset. Who knew? Not just a bit of aggressive mooing, which to be fair we might have expected. No, this was proper upset. They started coming for us.

I looked at Jim.

Jim looked at Wullie.

Wullie looked at me.

Paul looked at all of us. We'd forgotten about him.

I looked at Paul.

Jim looked at Paul.

Wullie looked at Paul.

We looked at him, but we can't, any of us, claim to have taken actual responsibility for him.

'RUN!!'

We ran. It's only when you start running that you realise how quick cows are. Oh, by the way, when this story was re-told for years after, these were bulls not cows. Who gets chased by cows? You get chased by bulls. You run with bulls. It's macho. It has a certain kudos to get chased by a bull, for you and the brave bull. It made us sound like manly men around many a camp fire.

Paul had to make his own mind up. He was only six. He chose to run with Wullie and me who, in an actual race for life, were heading for the top gate. I only knew Paul chose us as I could see him gaining on me out of the corner of my eye. The cows were also gaining fast though, and the top gate was uphill and further than it looked. We seemed to be doomed. Then a strange thing happened. Paul decided to change course and follow Jim to the bottom of the field. Instantly, the cows changed course too and followed him. Oh my God, they were after him. They were after our calf.

They are crafty. They do have a brain. They are pissed off, and they are catching up fast. Wullie and I watched helpless, and a little relieved if we're honest, from the top gate as the cows gained on our calf. Paul had built a slight lead due to the cows change of direction and with them having the turning circle of a Volvo. But Paul had too much drag. His head was slowing him down. He was proving to be less aerodynamic than a cow. It was touch and go.

There was so much aggressive, scary mooing and pounding and snorting. I mean all of them. Every cow was on it. They were determined to catch our little calf. In the film version of this it will cut ever quicker between panting cow (sorry bull), panting Jim, terrified Paul, back to bull (different one this time) as some dramatic music builds to a crescendo. Jim will reach the fence at the bottom of the field, turn and realise that Paul will be caught and killed (or at least have his arm broken) unless he does something heroic. Now we are just cutting between panting bull and panting Paul. Jim's okay. But, rather than save himself, he will turn back into the field, pick Paul up in his arms and carry him the last few yards throwing him over the fence to safety, whilst only just scraping under the barbed wire himself like Indiana Jones. Truth is Jim flew over that fence first and Paul only just made it under his own steam, sliding under the barbed wire held up by Jim. (it was the least he could do)

Paul was safe...if a little traumatised.

'I'm telling mammy on youse.' He bleated and cried.

He would learn though that you don't tell your mammy things she doesn't need to know.

'If you tell mother, we'll put you back in that field with the bulls.'

That seemed to do it. That and some counselling into his forties.

Tested to the limit you would think. So many chances to do the brave thing, yet we were all seemingly working on the old maxim that we didn't have to outrun the cows, we only had to outrun a six year old.

Bravery is a personal choice. We chose otherwise.

CHAPTER 9

Fire in the hole

We were unusually and idiotically brave around fire. We liked fire. We loved setting fires. I already hear some heads drop in judgment as, lighting fires is, in and of itself, not all that brave. So I am going in already knowing I am not coming out looking fresh faced. Bear with me. Don't judge us. Not yet. Plenty of time for that later when you have the full story. Also stories about lighting fires coming right after the cow chapter is starting to place this book in the horror section. I do feel an urge, now and again, to spend the rest of my days apologising to all cows personally, much as Governments are forced to do over past mistakes that weren't theirs. Though these mistakes were ours, so maybe an open letter in Farmer's Weekly ought to do it. That and a few less burgers.

I had spent that morning sitting an IQ test. Not just me, the whole class. I was at school, I didn't randomly set myself tests to pass the time. Nor was it a special test to check my individual intelligence, which is just as well given the upcoming events. I remember finding it very easy, so why I have not as yet received my Nobel Prize is beyond me. Anyway they gave us the afternoon off. Why? I have no idea. To rest our poor little brains after the huge effort maybe. If only we'd gone home for a lie down. Actually I am pretty sure our mother didn't believe I even had the afternoon off. You didn't get notes to take home or parent's evenings then. Teachers and parents kept themselves to themselves. An unexpected afternoon off school was only an irritant to the non-working (as she was then) mother, whose only job was to care for her children. So, we found ourselves outside and at a loose end. It was just Wullie and me initially,

Jim being older and at a different part of the school wasn't required to be tested that day.

What to do? What to do? Volunteer at soup kitchen? Bob a job? We weren't the Cub or Scouty type. That required discipline and following orders. We were mavericks. A little too maverick as it turned out.

Setting fire to the longy was a common pastime for us. It wasn't a farmer's field, it was wasteland. It was just some long grass, that in the damp west of Scotland climate, occasionally dried enough to warrant being burnt to a cinder. So we merrily set it on fire whenever we had the chance. Luckily for us, no animal life of any sort frequented the longy. No hedgehogs, mice, lapwings, beetles, rats, water voles, caterpillars, butterflies, dragonflies, sparrows, owls, kangaroos or wildebeest. None of those. So we didn't have to check or worry that we were continually destroying habitats, did we? Anyway they can all run or fly or hop. I am already drafting the letter that donates half the royalties of this book to the RSPCA.

Joe Graham

'Daredevil'

18 Denmilne Street, Easterhouse

Glasgow

No postcode..we didn't bother with those

Dear Sir/ Madam

You don't know me and with a bit of luck, you never will. I just wanted to check your thoughts on the burning of wildlife habitats. Would you say, for instance, that if you set fire to, oh I don't know, an area of long grass, somewhere near a canal, that you would be causing any untold damage to the wildlife, given they can all run or fly or hop. Is it your policy to send written notification to said wildlife that a fire of some sort is imminent, or is it best practice to NOT set the fire in the first place?

My personal understanding is that the natural warning signs are there. The crackling of the fire, the intense, life threatening heat and the excited whooping of nearby schoolboys, who have had nothing whatsoever to do with the setting of the potential fire. To set everyone's mind at rest, I was wondering if you could have a quick check of your records for the east end of Glasgow between 1964 and 1969 to see if any singed hedgehogs or lapwings with smoke damage were brought in. I am already assuming that any grasshoppers, or the like, caught up in any incident were pretty much toast and unlikely to make it to your door. But hey, we eat those like Smarties now and they are the protein food source of the future, so they are fair game I say.

Yours caringly (now)

Joe

Somehow Wullie had acquired two matches. Only two. Where from? Didn't ask. Not my business. Wasn't hard to work out, as everyone's parents smoked like chimneys. For us though, this was in the days long before two matches would have meant a sneaky fag. We were not into that in any way. Not for any health reasons. There weren't any. Cigarettes were cool then. Lots of lovely advertising and brightly coloured packets. No warnings. No indication that it was bad for you at all. Not in our world. Not then. We were too young. Our time to be cool would come and by the time it did, smoking wasn't cool any more.

Two matches only meant on thing. Fire! But it wasn't enough. No one could set the longy on fire with only two matches. It had never been done. Wullie wanted to try, but it was crazy thinking. But what else to do? Maybe it was the boredom. Maybe it was the easy IQ test making us think we were smarter than we actually were. Maybe it was the heat. It was hot and dry, and it wasn't hot or dry all that often. Ideal conditions. The perfect storm.

With everyone else at school, especially those who owned footballs, we were limited. We didn't have our own ball, so we couldn't even have a kickabout. You needed mates who had balls. Not balls, but balls. Not everybody had one, like they do now. If someone appeared on the street with a football, he was a hero forever, until it burst, then he was a nobody again. The power of the lad who owned the ball was ultimate. You played to his rules and to his timetable. When it was time for his tea or his bed, that was it. Some guys had the longest tea times in the world. It never took us that long to eat Spam or fish fingers. There's nothing to them. Some of these lads must have been having three course meals at the friggin' Ivy. The frustration of being in the middle of an exciting ten twenty oner*, (see rules below) when the ball owner gets shouted for his tea, which then turns out not to be tea at all, but a medieval banquet to rival anything served up to Henry VIII, is hard to describe to the modern child with his own ball.

We sat, looking longingly at the longy. Two matches. We had to plan. You don't just strike a match and make fire. Okay you do, but not a proper fire. You need to get a small fire going with dried grass and any paper you could find, usually old fag packets. They lay littered around everywhere. All sorts of litter lay littered around in days before the word litter was a dirty word...or even a word. Nobody took responsibility for littering, there were men for that. Men swept the streets then and did a bloody good job of it. If you didn't litter you would be doing that man out of a job. He wouldn't take kindly to that.

'Hey, where you gawn wi' that fag packet?'

'The potential litteree quickens his or her pace to escape.'

'Come back here you!'

The potential litteree takes off chased by a wee man and his street cleaning cart. Through alleyways, smashing past piles of empty, pointless cardboard boxes placed there for no reason, there was no Amazon remember.

'Ah'll deal wi' youse later.'

Eventually the wee man corners the culprit as he or she reaches a bin.

'What dae you think yur doing wi' that?'

'I put it in my pocket until found this suitable bin. I intended to and deposit it in there.'

'What am I, Scotch fucking mist? Drap it!'

'Sorry?'

'You hurd me. Put you hand in that pocket and slowly remove the fag packet. Keep the other haun where I can see it. Noo, drap the packet oan the grun.'

'But, that would be...'

'Drap it!'

'I can't.'

'I think you can. Dae as ah say or else. Slooowly.'

The litteree who has now about to become the litter-er drops the fag packet. Like swinging nun-chucks the wee man produces a brush and a shovel and sweeps it swiftly into his cart.

'Noo, on yur way, ya wee bastard. Let that be a lesson tae ye.'

We prepared dried grass torches to spread the fire quickly. But more often than not you could use up a whole box of matches to get it going properly. Two matches. We prepared our small fire and Wullie went into hamster hands mode. He was getting excited. Too excited as it turned out. He lit the first match. It blew out. Shit! One match. One match!! No one could set the longy on fire with only one match. It had never been done. It was about to be! We huddled together and Wullie struck the match. It lit. Our small fire was set and burning.

The rest all happened a bit quick. Like wildfire you might say. The grass torches did their job spreading the flames quickly. A little bit too quickly. Did I mention it was hot? The longy was up like a beacon in no time. Wullie's excited hamster hands were working overtime and if we knew what a high five was then, we would have been high fiving all over the place. We had no equivalent. What did we do before the high five? Handshakes all round? No. Certainly not man hugs. No man or boy was hugging every man he came into contact with, willy nilly, as we now do. So without Europe's influence and the high fiving USofA, Wullie and I were left to gaze at our incredible one match achievement with repressed pride and probably a congratulatory thank you note some weeks later. It's going to be hard in the film version to make this moment look as magical as it felt. I can see our glowing little faces. Wullie's half covered by his hamster pose and mine with an oddly angled hairline, recently cut by mother, and hands in a one-sided high five position long before anyone knew that it needed someone on the other end, as if waiting for social history to catch me up. One match. Two boys. One chance...to burn a lot of grass.

The irony of sitting an easy IQ exam at school in the morning and being given the afternoon off, which you then use to create a blazing inferno, was lost on me at that point. Nobody ever told me the result of that IQ test, but given the events of the rest of that day, I wasn't expecting a call from MENSA.

It should be pointed out that the longy fire that day fizzled out long before it had a chance to really affect the dog kennels situated at the far end of the longy. Oh, did I not mention the dog kennels? I thought I did. Pay attention. There were these dog kennels. Look, it's not as if we went around destroying every sign of animal life in the eastern half of Glasgow. It just looks like that. The dogs were fine. Besides most of them were greyhounds, so they could run really fast.

It was normally possible to contain any fire to the longy quite easily, with paths and bushes on one side and the canal road on the other. But isn't it funny how fire can spread unchecked? Isn't it?

It would be funny if we didn't already know how easily this could happen. Not our first Rodeo you might say.

All three of us, Jim included this time, were fully paid up pyromaniacs, by today's measure. I blame farmers. They were always burning fields. How were we to know there was a reason for that? It just looked like fun. It was fun, until our last fire. The bad fire. You know how kids get? Pushing boundaries.

This time it wasn't the longy that we targeted, it was the whole grassland area. The whole of Narnia. I say targeted. We didn't start the day intending to summon the hell fires of Hedes. It just sort of happened, like most things we did. You light a little fire, burn some grass. Then someone decides to burn some more grass, because who doesn't like to watch a small fire burn.

It occurs to me that the whole burning of grass reference is very sixties in a druggy, hippy sort of way. Wasn't that sort of grass. Wasn't that sort of sixties. No idea what a drug was, other than aspirin. Not a Paracetamol or an Ibuprofen or any of those, to be had. If aspirin couldn't fix it, then it wasn't fixable. It did seem to fix most things, so it does make you wonder if we need all the other stuff. There you have it, fifty years of medical science advances dismissed a thin blooded heartbeat. There was also Lucozade which was available as our main health drink. Not so daft now when you see its uses as an energy drink. Oh, and barley sugar sweets. Once you had all those, you would live forever, or until you discovered that cigarettes weren't quite the health sticks we all had them down for. So despite the deliberate setting of what was effectively a forest fires, without a forest, no drugs were taken or needed to come up with that idea.

With all three of us getting a bit carried away, before we knew it flames had spread beyond our buffer zone, which we had forgotten to create. Always safer to create a buffer zone so the fire can't spread too far. Obviously we didn't know what a buffer zone was and still don't really. Action had to be taken. With all the bravado of remembering we were Daredevils and the added convenience of ignoring the fact that we started it, we transformed from twisted firestarters into fully trained firemen. Things were going too far, but not to worry, we had this under control. All we had to do was beat it out with our sleeves and it would be fine. Who knew that plastic anoraks would simply melt in extreme heat? This was getting harder to explain never mind control.

Many of you from more temperate climates will be puzzled by the hot day and the anorak imagery. What were these boys doing wearing anoraks? Surely there is some historical inaccuracy. But you obviously have never lived in the west of Scotland. While I have been speaking things have taken a turn for the worse. As I was furiously beating the one single clump of grass with a disintegrating, quilted anorak sleeve. I looked over to see Wullie in full hamster hands mode. This wasn't excited hamster hands, this was fearful hamster hands. Terrified hamster hands. I turned slowly. Narnia was ablaze!

Then came the sirens. Oh my God, the sirens! It seems

other people must have noticed that half of Easterhouse was on fire. The fire engines roared along the canal road towards us. Followed, I think, by several helicopters carrying those large water bags and bringing up the rear was Red Adair and his full oil rig fire fighting team, who always have to shout loudly to each other over the sound of something. In this case very loud burning grass.

'We got a situation, Red.'

'Is it another oil rig blowout, Boots?' (I looked it up. His right hand man Asger "Boots" Hansen - research)

'It's a grass fire, Red.'

'A grass fire?'

'Not that kind of grass, Red.'

'What kind of grass?'

'You know...grass...grass.'

'Ahm a rootin' tootin' oil rig man, putting myself in harms way to cap burning oil rigs, I ain't got time for some diddly squat grass fire.'

'It's the biggest grass fire ever seen in these here parts.'

'Is that a fact?'

'No, I doubt it's actually a fact, Red.'

'Only one way to handle this kind of blaze, Boots.'

'What's that Red?

'Pass me my quilted anorak.'

The fear of seeing the approaching fire fighters, (It might have just been one engine, but I have seen a lot of disaster films since then and prone to exaggeration for effect) immediately transports me back to the bath scenario and it all begins to happen again, without the water this time. How the hell do we explain this?

Well, by lying of course. Lying and running. If anyone tried to pin it on us we had to get our stories straight. Some bigger boys had started fire and we, in full Daredevil mode and in an attempt to save the final lapwing's nest, east of Parkhead from extinction, had to intervene. Even under extreme parental interrogation, we would not crack. Daredevils do not crack.

'Where are these bigger boys?'

'They perished in the fire.'

You don't die in a fire, you perish.

'No bodies were found.'

'Did you see the fire?'

'Why is your face all black, apart from the tracks of tears and snotters?'

'We tried to save a sparrow.'

'Lapwing.'

'Sorry, lapwing.'

'Where is this lapwing?'

'We tired, we failed. Perished.'

'What happened to your anorak sleeves?'

It should be pointed out that the actual interrogation and fallout from the anorak sleeves themselves was cataclysmic, and I am making it sound here like part of a controlled questioning. Our parents did not care about the fire; the survival of the native lapwing; or about us smelling like fire, we smelled like that all the time. But we had ruined two perfectly serviceable anoraks. In Wullie's case it was a jumper sleeve ruined by two tightly clenched, beating hamster hands. I suspect he got out of that easier than we did once again. Maybe he just complained less than we did. We did continue to wear the same anoraks, sleeves and all, for quite some time after.

'I said, what happened to your anorak sleeves?'

'Nothing.'

'They've melted.'

'You will buy cheap anoraks, mother.'

'How were we to know that we would be caught in such an inferno and that our anoraks would not be up to the job.'

'You started the fire, didn't you?'

'We don't start fires, we put them out, like this one.'

'It's what Daredevils do.'

'Dare what?'

'Nothing. No-one. Nothing.'

Almost a sudden Peter Parker type moment, revealing his identity and putting his aunt May in harm's way.

'You started the fire, didn't you?'

'Didn't you?'

'No!'

'Didn't you?'

'Don't press us mother, there are things a mother doesn't need to know for her own safety.'

'Is that a lapwing squashed on that sleeve?'

....

*A ten twenty-oner was simply a football game of two halves, with an indeterminate number of players on each side (a heady mixture of George Bests and Emile Heskeys, with the odd Stephen Hawking thrown in). The first half is decided by whichever team reaches ten goals first, with the second half naturally played out till one team reaches twenty one goals. Given the length of time and commitment required *for a ten twenty-oner, players can often get sucked into one, unknowingly, by it starting out as a five-elevener – The first half is decided by whichever team reaches five goals...You get the gist. This appears to be a much more manageable contest and one which will allow you to get on with the rest of your life, but most players will succumb to an eventual ten twenty-oner once the tenth goal goes in and nobody wants to lose. So it's best not to make plans that weekend. The average ten twenty-oner could last a whole day and were often played way past sunset, assuming the ball owner had the foresight to purchase a white ball. Goals were disputed long and hard without the benefit of slow motion replay or goal line technology - or jumper technology, as we would have required then. The goal line itself never proved that much of an issue. The tricky part was determining whether a ball had crossed between the width of two jumpers. Jumpers not being all that tall and goalpost like. More often than not, these heated disputes would end with the ball owner taking his ball home, if the decision didn't go his way, so abandoning the match. It was always prudent to award such decisions to the team containing the ball owner.*

CHAPTER 10

Beyond the edge of the world

Our world was small, but there were times we needed to see more. We all have a desire to travel and explore and we were no different. Planes weren't invented yet, but we weren't ready for them anyway. There was also no promise of a gap year to look forward to. That wasn't about to happen anytime soon. Even now I'm not entirely sure how teenagers got that one past their parents.

'So, I was thinking father...of taking a gap year.'

'What's one of those?'

'You know, take a year off. Stop school and all that tiring learning and go see the world, or watch telly or something.'

'A year off?'

'What do you say? Exciting isn't it? And best of all you get to pay for it.'

'You're eleven.'

'I think it would help me grow as a person to experience different cultures. I feel that I have taken school as far as I can go. That IQ test was really easy, so they aren't stretching me anyway.'

'Great, you can work in the shipyards with me, labouring for a year.'

'I can't work in a shipyard, I'm eleven.'

'It would help you grow as a person.'

'I wasn't thinking of working.'

'I bet you weren't. Get back to school and shut up!'

If we wanted to explore we would have to organise our own

expeditions and venture beyond our borders to discover new worlds. Yes I know Christopher Columbus and those dudes had sort of discovered most of the known world by then, but we hadn't. What was beyond our normal world was just as new and exotic as America would have been to Chris and his compagnos.

At this point in history America was already stuffing itself with burgers on the way to its current and disastrously obese future. By that I mean the sixties, not 1492 when Chris landed wherever he landed. America must have been secret eating because we didn't know what they were up to. They kept it well hidden. We never saw them eat a burger in Bonanza. They all looked shiny and healthy. Except Hoss. Even a man the size of Hoss didn't get that way from eating junk food. It was glandular with Hoss. He worked a long hard day on the ranch, dealt with interlopers and common bad guys, got Little Joe out of sticky situations and went home ans sat down to a healthy, yet hearty meal with the whole family. Junk food didn't exist in our world. Not quite true I suppose if you consider deep frying everything to be an unhealthy way to go, but you know what I mean. We had to see what was out there. Not America, we knew exactly what that was like. In the countryside they all rode horses, didn't like Indians and had big ranches; In the cities they were all private investigators, fighting crime.

We had to set our binoculars just past the canal. The exotic and as yet unexplored land of Ballieston.

There were no garden gates to hold us. No gardens at all really and no fear of what might happen to us. Ballieston and more specifically our end goal, Calderpark Zoo, was all of two miles away-ish. We didn't know it was two miles away. We didn't really know how far two miles was. What child of 8-10 years old has any real concept of distance? It was quite far away we knew that. But we also knew from contacts on the street, that there was a way to get in the zoo free. A hole in the fence. Let's face it, what intrepid exploring Daredevil would not travel to the end of the world if there was a chance of getting through a hole in a fence for free to anywhere. There was no chance of ever visiting such an exotic location without this golden opportunity.

I know lots of kids and families went to zoos, but not us. It was not on our family social calendar. My dad did not get in from a hard days welding at the shipyards of Greenock, covered in dirt, his jumper full of holes from the welding sparks, brightly exclaiming 'Hands up who wants to go the zoo?' Weekends were taken up with dad popping to the bookies and back again several times on Saturday and with mass on Sunday. Probably more to it than that, but that was the gist and everything else revolved around those. Besides zoos cost money. Betting on horses didn't. That was free. Bear in mind a ten twenty-oner can take a whole weekend, so going to zoos wasn't even on our radar. We were far too busy to ask. Our social calendar was one holiday a year, where we always spent the first few hours:

A. Finding the nearest Catholic church. Not a Protestant one. That wont do at all. We might be on holiday, but we're not savages.

B. Finding the nearest bookie and standing for hours outside the bookies waiting for dad. I'm sure there were many times he forgot we were there.

Not sure who our contact was on the whole hole thing. I think Wullie played that one close to his chest. Nobody blabs openly about this kind of thing. Once word gets out, the hole gets fixed and it's sayonara free ride. So better not to know. Not to ask. Egghead wanted to come but he's a blabber. Or a yopper as we would say. He would yop on us. He would crack if anyone asked where we were going. It wasn't an easy decision as he could carry stuff, but it was safer for him if he didn't know.

'Where are you going?'

'Nowhere.'

'You don't need to know.'

'Can I come?'

'No.'

'It's too dangerous.'

'I like danger.'

'Since when?'

'I spit on danger.'

He spat, but it didn't come out right and dribble down his chin like an eggy soldier. Not a good look or a good sign if you can't actually spit on danger. Danger would not be challenged by a dribbling chin.

It was dangerous. We thought it was dangerous. There was risk involved. A lifetime on the Lam if we were caught sneaking in. We had no room for baggage. Even though I suspect that to Jim and Wullie...I was baggage. I often was. No matter, we had no room for excess baggage. It didn't stop him pleading his case.

'Danger is my middle name.'

It wasn't. Nobody had middle names, apart from all the people who had middle names, but nobody asked your middle name. Nobody wanted to know. The only middle name I knew was my dad's; 'Parks'. James Parks Graham. Kinda cool. Anyway if we all had middle names there would be no room for your Confirmation name. Your unofficial middle name. Everybody wanted to know that.

'Hello, I'm Joe.'

'Nice to meet you, Joseph. What's your Confirmation name?'

'Does it matter?'

'It matters to God.'

'Nobody uses it.'

'God knows you by it.'

Does he? Does he really? Because it is usually some common Saint name. Mine is James I think. Which is going to confuse the bejesus out of God, because that's my brother's actual name, so when I get there God thinks I'm him and thinks he is Mark or Matthew or someone. I can't remember his Confirmation name. He will, so I might need another addendum. I don't think people do it now. Can you imagine some of the Confirmation names that would crop up now? Nobody is going to settle for Mary or Joseph when they can have Buzz or Chardonnay. You will notice I said 'when' I get there, not 'if'. Despite all the harm we might have unintentionally caused to various life forms. That is because we are Roman Catholic and even the most lapsed RC will still get there as long as he confesses all his sins in the end. So no point in continually confessing or going to mass if you can store it all up at the end and settle it then. Unless you get hit by a bus unexpectedly. Those life forms, by the way, are of course by default, Protestant and as we were led to understand it, not going to Heaven. So no bees or cows or lapwings or sparrows, unless they convert.

Danger wasn't Egghead's middle name. We didn't even know his first name.

'Danger is my middle name.'

'Okay, come on then.'

'Will I get back for tea time?'

'I doubt it. Calderpark Zoo is miles away.'

'Calderpark Zoo?'

'There's a hole in a fence.'

I yopped.

'I can't go there, my dad will kill me.'

Of course he will. Our dad would kill us too, but that's the point. You don't tell your dad anything. Christopher Columbus didn't tell his dad where he was going. Do you think for one second his dad would have let him take off around the world, when he didn't even know if there was a world? Are you kidding? His dad would have killed him. At least we knew Calderpark Zoo existed. I say that. I had never seen it. Only heard of it. It might not have been where Wullie thought it was.

Wullie knew the way. There was no map. I think someone made Wullie eat it after telling him about the hole, before realising that Calderpark Zoo had many visitors and probably printed it's own maps. Everyone knew where it was. Not everyone knew about the hole though.

One intrepid journey later, we were there...at the hole. True enough our informant was right. Right behind the reptile house. Perfect cover. A flimsy wire fence with a big hole. We camouflaged our faces and put on our night goggles. Sorry, too many films again.

All our experience of the world beyond Narnia was going to be needed here to avoid detection and capture. We knew how to handle ourselves in many situations. We were allowed out. I fact as mentioned before, we were barely allowed in. This one felt further than most places we had been because of the unknown...the danger....the long bloody walk there and especially back.

Most places were a short train or bus ride, so they didn't

seem quite as far out of our comfort zone as this expedition. Although it reads like we never left the surrounding streets, there were other places that were very much part of our world. Places further away than the zoo. Further flung places that weren't mysterious or out of our comfort zone. This is because we transported ourselves there and back without having to encounter the world in between. A bit like wormholes. Tears in the fabric of time. Or buses and trains as we called them. The zoo and the lands in between bus and train routes were a leap into the unknown.

Swimming was a regular Saturday wormhole outing. It's all coming back to me why we never had time for zoos. I say swimming. I couldn't actually swim. The baths at Coatbridge were three stops on the train. I'm pretty sure mother gave us train fare to make that journey legally, but that would have been too easy. Our preferred method was to rush past the ticket man on the gate declaring confidently that 'Our dad was coming right behind us.' Leap onto the train and be gone into the night.. or Saturday morning. It always seemed to work. It worked like clockwork until one day Jim and I were getting on the train and our dad was actually coming right behind us, or so we thought. As we boarded the train, he followed on just in time for the doors to close on us and the train to take off without him.

Nooooooo!! Daaaaaaaddy!!!

You have never seen such panic. Jim and I cried, wailed and sobbed as if being prised from our loving father's arms onto a train bound for the concentration camps. Hey, we didn't know. It was possible. There was a cold war on, as I remember noting in my, all knowing, diary.

It was the same train we always took on our own. Dad was never normally with us anyway. So why the big greet? Not sure where we were going that day, but dad wasn't taking us swimming I know that. Why would he want to sit on a bench for an hour watching some kids turn blue? Parents are too concerned with their children potentially drowning now and feel they have monitor their every move, poised to save their life at any sign of danger.

The only danger. I was in was from hypothermia and chlorine poisoning. Wullie and Jim could swim and so would jump in and splash off doing swimmy things with all the confidence of Aquaman and his sidekick Aqualad (seriously). That's how it looked to me. They did the same things with bikes. I couldn't ride a bike either, so they would set off on biking adventures, whenever they managed to borrow bikes, leaving me to play with myself. Not that.

I am beginning to see that I had no boyhood skills whatsoever.

I spent an hour in freezing water clinging, blue lipped, to the edge at the shallow end praying for our band colour to be called so I could get out.

'Will all those with white bands please leave the pool?'

'Damn. Make it yellow..Yellow!'

'Will all those with...red bands please leave the pool?'

'Noooooo!'

I wont survive another session. The pool attendant has just emptied what seems like a gallon of chlorine into the pool. Somebody must have peed again. Not me. Not this time. They didn't care then. Didn't filter it in. Just emptied buckets of it in there while everyone was still swimming. Only those clinging to the edge too terrified to move or be splashed would be affected, so I guess they saw me as collateral damage. My eyes are stinging now. Burning. Red rimmed and puffy. My lips have gone from blue to purple. Veins are spreading across my palid skin. I look like someone washed up on a beach three weeks after drowning at sea. Everyone is beginning to look at me and wonder why I'm not moving. Now I feel self-conscious. I have to do something. I have to move. So spurred on by the overriding desire not to be a laughing stock and not to die right there in Coatbridge baths, the most magical thing happens. It's like a miracle. The kind of thing that might happen at Lourdes every day of the week, not Coatbridge baths.

I begin to swim.

One width. Easy does it. Lengths were out the question. Swimming pools are deep. Did you know that? Then another width. Oh yes, look at me go. There is no way anyone can tell that I am actually walking on the bottom. No way! My above water swimming technique is just too good, too natural, and water isn't all that see through, is it? I kept this technique up for years until I finally learned to swim at age 13. About same time I learned to ride the bike my granny won at bingo. That year sounds like it could be a whole new book on its own, but I think that was it.

'Will all those with...yellow bands please leave the pool?'

'Yes!!'

Quickly change to mock sadness.

'Oh no, really? That went quick. I was really enjoying that. Curse you mister announcer man.'

It felt like a lifetime. We always had chicken soup from the vending machine after. I think it was a machine. The hypothermia might have made me delirious, so it could have been a drip inserted by paramedics. I loved that chicken soup though. Never tasted anything like it since. Never really liked swimming all that much since either.

I much preferred our bus trips to Parkhead. We were

brought up Catholic of course, so that means in footballing terms, you support Glasgow Celtic. No choice. No say. Full blown religious segregation was the tolerant attitude of the day. Not too much has changed in the world.

'Can I support Rangers, daddy?'

'No son, you cant.'

'Why not? They have that Jim Baxter and he's a great player.'

Or a top, top player as we know have to call them. Being top isn't enough and very soon, unless they come up with a new word, being top top isn't going to cut it. We will have to keep adding 'tops'.

'Why not? They have that Jim Baxter and he's a top, top, top top, top top, top player.'

'He may well be a top, top, top top, top top, top player son, but he's a Proddie.'

'But I wanted a shirt with his name on it for Christmas.'

'For Christmas? For the baby Jesus' birthday, you want a Proddie football shirt?'

'Is that not good, daddy?'

'No, it is not good.'

'Why not?'

'Because the baby Jesus wont like it'

'If I ask Santa, will he bring me one.'

'No son, he wont.'

'Why daddy? Why?'

'Because son, Santa is a Catholic.'

Parkhead it was. Only one way into the ground. Simple. You walk up to a strange man ask him to be your daddy. Effectively. In a paranoid post Saville world that is going to sound odd, and not quite how we put it. Kids got in free if their parent or guardian lifted them over the turnstile, and as we more often than not went to football without parental shackles, we always had to ask a grown up to lift us over said turnstiles. Nobody ever refused. It was the done thing. In we go and off down the terraces singing pro IRA songs with all the gusto of a Martin McGuiness surprise birthday party.

You guessed it, we didn't know about the IRA then either. We were too young and they hadn't yet started the full on atrocities of the late sixties/early seventies. We chanted their historical praises with all the joy and conviction we would later offload onto Slade's 'Cum on Feel the Noize'.

Saturday is when it all happened. If it wasn't football or swimming, it was something else. That was always the day for action and adventure beyond the confines of Denmilne Street. Never Sunday. Because nothing opened on a Sunday. Sunday was the day you spent in limbo waiting for it to be Monday again. After you had been to mass of course; done the altar boy thing and missed out on any fun those lucky heathens were having. It was the Lord's day. A day of rest. A day to relax, unwind, take it easy. Nobody could shop or go anywhere for entertainment, because the world was shut! In other words, the most boring day you could possible imagine, where the only shining light at the end of that long, dark Sunday tunnel...was Monday.

I don't know the figures, but the suicide rate must have trebled on a Sunday. We criticise the 24 hour culture that we have now and yes, we may have gone too far the other way, but just think of the number of lives Asda is saving by simply allowing people to buy a George T- shirt for £4.99 every Sunday. I'm starting to feel a bit suicidal just thinking about it and it drags up feelings of my only other moment of suicidal thought.

Bambi's fault.

Our other regular excursion was the Shettleston State, our closest cinema and another of those short wormhole bus rides away. Saturday mornings queuing round the block to see Zulu is a fairly typical memory of just about everyone. Well documented and not very interesting. This particular Saturday though, Bambi was out. The level of excitement about this was off the chart. For many years I assumed, wrongly, that this was because it was a brand new release and the whole world was buzzing about Walt Disney's latest creation. If anything better illustrates the way the world and our viewing habits have changed, then I have yet to experience it, because this bloody film was over twenty years old...then! Why were we so excited? What was so dull about the whole sixties that a cartoon from 1942 had us all wetting our pants. But wet our pants we did. Not literally. Not then.

We had to see it. Mother must have been feeling particularly generous that day, or more keen than usual to get rid of us, but she gave us the money to go see Bambi. Bambi! This is three brave Daredevils that I have, so far, attempted to paint with all the rugged charm of Huckleberry Finn. Three brave Daredevils skipping to the bus stop to see Bambi.

Well, anyway it turns out that not only did we have to see it, so did everyone else. It was completely sold out. You would think that Bambi himself was putting in a public appearance, such was the fervour. Obviously his mother couldn't make it. Not that any of us knew why at that point.

We can't get in. Queue as we did. Try as hard as we did. No way. Not today kids. So, we simply trudge back on to the bus, head home and give mother the money back for the tickets and go build a new den or light a fire.

At least, that's what we should have done.

We didn't. We put our collective heads together and decided that as mother had already given us the money and was obviously happy to take the financial hit, we could simply spend the money on sweets and treats for ourselves. Where was the harm? And besides, we had a wonderful sting in that tail, that would keep everyone happy. I don't know how much perfume costs these days. Seems to be a lot. So, either perfume stocks and shares had dropped to an all time low, or we had bought our poor mother the cheapest, shittiest bottle of watery crap you could imagine, as a sweetener for spending the money we were supposed to use to see Bambi. I would like to build a case for sweet innocent young boys simply doing a good thing and not getting what was wrong with the scenario, but I think the actual act of buying the perfume, or whatever the hell that was, suggests we were not entirely comfortable with our actions that day.

Turns out we were right not to be entirely comfortable with our actions that day. Mother went absolutely ballistic. We had seen her angry before. She did on occasion get the slipper out as a punishment. But that was okay. For one thing, it never hurt and was just a visual aid for mother to indicate her anger. We knew that and I think she did too. Brandishing a slipper is a great way to tell your children that all is not right in the world. On those slippery occasions, we pretty much deserved whatever was coming. I am 100% sure of that. Mother also had a tendency to leave home quite a lot when it all got too much, she would don her coat and announce her intention to leave home forever and storm out. Got us every time. We would forlornly watch her disappear down the road, from our bedroom window knowing deep inside she had probably just gone to the shops. Like last time. But there was always that chance that we had driven her out for good this time. Gone.

Hopped a Greyhound to Pittsburgh and never seen again, and it would be up to us to explain that to dad when he got home.

'Where's your mother?'

'Who?'

'Mother. Your mum. Where is she?'

'We thought you had her.'

'I've been at work.'

'Was she not at work with you?'

'In a shipyard? Welding?'

'Hey dad, it is the sixties.'

'What does that mean?'

'You know sexual liberation and all that.'

'You're ten. You don't even know what that is.'

'She's at the shops.'

'How long has she been at the shops?'

'Six hours.'

'She's run away again, hasn't she?'

So it wasn't her anger that got to me that day. Or her obvious lack of appreciation for the marvelous gift we had bought her, out of her own money. It was how upset she was. She probably had that money earmarked for other things, but she let us have it that day and we let her down by rubbing really cheap perfume into her wounds. I wanted to die. So it's just as well we never saw the depressing load of nonsense that is Bambi or else I think I might have thrown myself in the nolly and ended it all. Though by the sounds of it if we had seen it, I might have thrown myself in the nolly, so it's a chicken egg thing.

Wullie's hippy style mum was obviously a lot more liberal, gullible or Wullie simply lied his arse off and told her he had seen Bambi. He certainly didn't appear to have the same problem when he got home. Thanks for the heads up Wullie. Why didn't we just tell her Bambi was great? I am pretty sure we didn't think for whatever reason, that we could pull of that level of deceit. Oh how I wish we had. We lied about everything else, and nobody knew the plots of films then, even twenty year old bloody cartoons.

'How was the film?'

'Great.'

'What is it about?'

'Bambi.'

'I guessed that. What happens?'

'Bambi lives in a wood and stuff happens...and stuff.'

'What stuff?'

'Bad guys come into the wood and Bambi and his friend the...badger have to fight them with karate skills...and knives.'

'Bambi has a knife?'

'Yes. And a gun. The bad guys want to chop a tree down and Bambi is...adamant that they shouldn't, so he...'

'...Shoots them?'

'Yes. No. Yes. But they shoot too and a big gun battle happens between the bad guys and all the woodland creatures. Squirrels with machine guns and a rabbit with a bazooka.'

'Does Bambi win?'

'Yes, after a lot of shooting and fighting.'

'Is that how his mother dies?'

'His mother dies!!???'

Partly as a matter of principle and partly because I have seen tiny snippets on R**f H****s' Cartoon Time, which look rubbish, I have never seen Bambi all the way through. Apologies if that was a plot spoiler. Apologies too, if you don't know who R**f H****s is, but we aren't allowed to mention Rolf Harris anymore.

We made it to the hole in the zoo fence. We survived the journey without realising what it is we had survived. The world in between beyond our normal streets had rules, borders. You don't simply walk out of your own area. These areas belonged to someone. To gangs. The Drummy and the Young Den-Toi spring mostly to mind. Names designed to strike fear into you. These were daubed large on walls to leave you in no doubt as to whose territory you were about to enter at your peril. God help you if you wandered into another territory and they find out you are not from there, so you can see the danger in our two mile walk to Calderpark Zoo. I don't think we fully thought through how many gang territories we would be crossing. Brave? No. Stupid? I think so. But we got away with it.

I looked up other gang names just for Easterhouse; Skinheads; Aggro; Bal-Toi; Provvy. All terrifying and only a tiny sample of the hundreds of gangs that laid claim to their few streets of territory in Glasgow.

Happy days.

No need to worry about all that. Not till we have to get back. For now we have to make our move. Get into the zoo. Wullie's hamster hands were on full alert. Is he excited? Is he shitting himself. Hamster hands covered a multitude of emotions and most of his face. But this was his idea and he was going first. He did that thing with two fingers and a shakey fist that the SAS do just before going in. Nobody knows what that means. So we all just ran. As we passed the reptile house we broke into a casual walk.

We're in.

The guards didn't suspect a thing. Yes, we thought there were guards. With all those dangerous animals, there are bound to be guards. Guards that didn't know there was a breach in the perimeter. There were no guards. Nothing to guard. It was rubbish. I have seen pictures of the zoo since and it does look like they had lions, tigers, rhinos and all that. Reptiles of course. But I have no wondrous recollection of seeing my first tiger and deciding to dedicate my life to saving the endangered species of the world. No epiphany to become David Attenborough. Nobody wanted to be David Attenborough then. David Attenborough wasn't even David Attenborough then. I mean, of course, he was David Attenborough, but he wasn't 'David Attenborough'. It was the gorillas that made him. He was nobody before that. Well, he was David Attenborough, but you know what I mean.

Lions are always boring in zoos, so I totally get why I don't remember them. Rhinos? A lot of mud usually and they don't do much either, except when they are charging and trying to kill you. I suspect though, that having seen pictures of Calderpark Zoo in its later years, that those particular rhinos had long since given up the will to live, never mind kill. It really wasn't a great advert for keeping animals in zoos. Not exactly memorable. Bizarrely enough, the only animal I do remotely remember... and this is a zoo don't forget...is a black swan.

Yes, they had a swan and it was black. Wow! Never seen anything so exotic in all my life. Or anything so dangerous. Think about it. Think about the damage a normal white swan can do. Well, this was a black swan with a red bill. All that effort and risking our lives and all I can bring to mind is a swan. I wonder is Big Chris was similarly underwhelmed when he got to the Brave New World.

'What was it like Chris?'

'It was alright.'

'Alright? Surely it was better than that?'

'I don't really remember much about it.'

'You are supposed to remember, it's why we bloody sent you. They are undiscovered worlds, surely there were sights no man has seen before?'

'A couple of unusual trees and some nice beaches.'

'We got beaches here. What else?'

'It's hard to remember, it's been a long journey.'

'Is it worth everyone in the whole civilised world upping sticks and moving there?'

'I wouldn't bother.'

'What about mythical beasts? Are those lands not swarming with beasts and wildlife that until now no man could even imagine.'

'They do have black swans.'

To be fair this was no ordinary swan, this was a ninja swan!

CHAPTER 11

The shadow of the tree

With nothing much to hang about for it was time to head back home. The thrill was long gone. Anyway the height of the thrill was, as it turns out, getting in unnoticed. I suppose we expected there to be actual thrills to be had in the actual zoo, but alas, no. Unless you count the Ninja swan.

There was a choice to be made. Back through the streets and about seven gang territories, that we should have thought about on the way there, but didn't....or the countryside route over the railway track. Still technically in gang territory, but much less patrolled. This is how the VonTrapp's got out of Austria, so it was bound to work for us.

We had become irrationally jittery about the street option. Not that irrational in point of fact. Probably more irrational not to have considered it a dangerous route on the way there.

Country route it is. Potential gangs, the fading light and uncaged ninja swans were preying on our minds. Daredevil tactics would not work if we encountered real people. Especially real people intent on beating you up, or worse. I say we decided on the country route, but I don't recall knowing it was the country route when we set off. Jim and Wullie no doubt fronted it out pretending they knew, but I think when civilization ran out, they were every bit as surprised as I was that we were heading into countryside. We were used to countryside. Our bit of countryside. But the trouble with fields and trees is that they all look the same and don't have nameplates on them, or, to be fair, warning signs threatening to kill you if you dare pass them. Where does the countryside end though? It can go on forever.

I was praying Wullie had one of those shoes with a compass in the heel, because I have no idea how he knew where we were going. Thinking about it, not sure a compass would have helped. You have to know which direction you actually want to head in for a compass to be of any use. Like many decision this was out of my hands. I was the youngest so I simply followed and assumed everyone else knew what they were doing.

You can see that a lot of things happened in spite of my presence, and not as a direct result of it. I never seemed to be a take charge kind of guy, but I was the youngest, so that wasn't my job. I didn't have a job beyond creating the double D Daredevil logo and membership cards.

I scrawled a symbol on an old science notebook. The hard backed blue type with red spine. Not the cheap, shitty coloured jotters. Oh no, this was serious. This had to last. It had to be recorded for posterity for future generation to learn form I wonder where it is now? The notebook would record our exploits. Our code of honour would be written up in this revered journal, that was once Wullie's big brother's homework notebook. He had moved up a year and he said we could use it if we tore out the pages he'd used for his physics homework.

As I held up the science notebook, we looked in awe at the finished symbol, a rough, intertwined double D symbol, and knew we would honour this code forever.

My design skills honed much later in life were obviously always there from the start and the Daredevils needed me. They needed drawings of costumes that we couldn't wear; lists of powers we didn't possess; and a mission statement, scrawled in pencil, on the back of the membership cards, of our intention to help the weak and stand up for good in the world. Intentions that we would never really fulfill, but no less nobly intended for that. We would fight the good fight where we could...with smaller boys than us. We weren't stupid.

The DD membership cards were a permanent record of our right to be a Daredevil. Flash that at some wrong 'un and he or she would surely run for the hills. The card would strike fear into our enemies. I say permanent, this is before lamination was even thought about. Pretty sure that was a result of the space programme too like everything else of any use. Science fiction at best. Though we could dream.

'You know what would help make those cards more permanent?'

'Writing them in our own blood?'

'No, that would just make reprints more painful. What I am talking about is...lamination.'

'Is that a place?'

'It's a thing. Very thin plastic stuck over the card.'

'Then you wont see the card.'

'Very thin.'

'How thin?'

'Thinner than a human hair.'

'How thin is that?'

'Pretty thin.'

'What colour?'

'No colour, see through.'

'Very thin plastic you can see through?'

'Yes, and it's sticky too?'

'Very thin plastic you can see through even though it's covered in glue?'

'Invisible glue.'

'I was thinking of sticking them to the back of a Kellogg's

Corn Flakes packet.'

'Or that.'

Corn Flakes packet it was. The thickest known card available to the boy on the street then and the ideal way to make a rigid, indestructible membership card. Stick two sides back to back using that fishy smelling glue, so that you can draw on both sides and voila; a slightly dingy grey card that was almost impossible to write on with pencil. But a powerful weapon for good.

Like any journey, the way back always feels longer and more miserable. There is no anticipation, and with each passing identical tree or field we were moving out of our comfort zone. It just seemed to be taking bloody ages. Darkness was beginning to fall and although it would be some time, days maybe, before our parents would bother to send up a warning flare, it was becoming obvious that Wullie didn't have a compass in his shoe. He was winging it and wasn't altogether sure where we were. Or where north was. We were passing a forest...okay a wood...okay a clump of trees. Everything was bigger then, cut me some poetic slack.

I was starting to imagine gangs of Ninja swans silently tracking us to move in for the kill. Swinging through trees even though they can actually fly. Flying isn't really a quiet graceful affair for a swan though. They do make a lot of fuss getting up or down. So the swinging Ninja killer swans had the right idea. Who was I kidding? The swans were a light-hearted distraction for what I was really I imagining. I was imagining werewolves. I hated werewolves. It was getting dark. We were off the path. Okay we were on the road, but it felt like we had strayed off the path – and you don't stray off the path. I don't know what it is about werewolves that really put the shits up me. I think it's that they can be real. I know they're not real, but compared to Dracula or the Mummy or any of those other supposedly scary things, that we had presented to us as the ultimate in fear, werewolves were the most likely to be possible. Of course they are!! They are wolves, who like to bite you and turn you into a wolf. The fact that they can be people too isn't even the point, because as people, by day, they are nice and friendly, so you would never know, until they transformed into a werewolf, mauled you and then you are one too. Too late. No choice. All plausible. Zombies weren't a big thing then. Very popular now, but Dracula and the Mummy were sort of zombies and not that scary.

What makes it scary is not the werewolf hunting you, but the idea that you could be the werewolf. We were still in an era of Peter Cushing and Christopher Lee, before he became a wizard. There weren't any scary people running around with ice hockey masks or chainsaws. I suspect it took about three men to carry the kind of chainsaws that they had then. That's three men all deciding at the same time that they had similar murderous intent and being free on the same night, to go out and about taking turns killing random strangers. The lightweight chainsaw meant you could figure out how to kill on your own. There were no paedophiles either.

A bold statement of untruth considering how we are now discovering that just about everyone back then was a paedophile. Who knew? Indeed. The point is, it wasn't a thing we feared or had even heard of.

I didn't mention werewolves to the others. They were too busy whistling. I now recognise this a dry nervous whistle, but at the time was just further annoyed that I couldn't whistle. Lots of things I couldn't do and whistling was always one of them. Still can't. I can fake a sort of breathing in whistle, but not a full blowing out one or those high pitched finger whistles.

The main reason I decided not to ever have a sheepdog. That and the fact any dog is only one dark thought away from being a werewolf. Can't get them out of my mind.

There are good reasons not to mention the werewolf fear out loud though. Jim and Wullie may have scoffed at the fact that they're not real..even though they plausibly are...or have been just as terrified at the mention of them. Worse still, it can also set off a conversation suggesting things more terrifying than a werewolf, if there is such a thing. What if the thing they dare not speak, was worse than mine.

'Has anybody thought that there might be, oh I don't know, werewolves in the woods.'

'Werewolves?'

'Sssh.. don't say it too loud.'

'You don't want to worry about werewolves.' Jim reassured me.

'Oh really? Thanks bro.'

'It's ghosts you want to worry about.'

Ghosts were worse. What if we start telling ghost stories? That could escalate to heart attack territory. Thankfully I didn't mention it and Jim and Wullie carried on with an increasingly drying whistle.

We were on our own.

Our parents would not be scouring the streets looking for us just because it was dark. Mothers only came seeking you out for one reason and one reason only. To shout you in for your tea. Parents seemed to instinctively know that they had to feed us at certain intervals. It must have been something they learned from their parents. Genetic almost. But once we were fed, we were sent out to play again. Our parents didn't want to see us again till bedtime. Until you were the last child wandering the streets, and going home to bed was your only option, other than sleeping rough.

'What are you doing in?'

'It's midnight.'

'I thought I told you to go out to play?'

'You did. That was six hours ago.'

'Where are all your mates?'

'In their jammies, tucked up in bed being read the brand new children's best seller, James and the Giant Peach.'

'You better come in then.'

'Thanks.'

Ah, the warm welcome home. But before your arse touched a sofa, or you could defrost your frozen fingers on the three bar electric fire. The only one by the way.

'Bed.'

'What about a story?'

'A story?'

'You know, reading me a story.'

'Reading you a story?'

'Yes.'

'Can't you read?'

'Yes.'

'Read your own story, then. Lights out in five minutes.'

I'll read a comic.'

We never did stories. Just time for a quick re-read of the 'Oor Wullie' Christmas annual. (different Wullie - no relation. This one was a cartoon)

Being last in was always a better option than being first. No one wanted to be called in to bed. What an embarrassment to be the first to be shouted by your mum for bedtime. A cry would ring out over the darkened street, carried in the wind to the dark patch of scrubland we were playing on.

'Angus! Time for bed.'

I'm using an obvious pseudonym for this. It isn't right to use a real person for such an indignity.

'Angus! Bedtime!'

'But mum, I'm playing.'

Imagine it. It's a ten twenty-oner. You know the rules. It's pitch black. No one can even see the ball anymore, but its 20-20. Next goal wins. No one is giving in. There might not even be a ball. There were times I am sure we were running around slide tackling, twenty minutes after the guy whose ball it was had gone home with it.

'I said bed! Now!'

'Five minutes.'

'Now.'

'Two minutes'

'Now!!'

'One minute.'

'I said now.'

'Ten seconds.'

'Do I have to come down there?'

Most mothers had no appetite for negotiation in these circumstances. They knew that if you didn't come now, they would be unlikely to ever see you again. That would be it. Gone, forever. A lost boy living in Neverland with all the other lost boys who never came in when they were shouted in for bed. Or, if they had just been a little patient, Angus would have been there in about five minutes. Being a parent subsequently,

I know that a lot of the panic and timing was down to not missing you favourite programme on the telly....and the lack of invention of any sort of recording device as yet.

On the field of play, panic sets in. It's like one of those football matches where no one makes a bloody effort for eighty eight minutes and then, as one, all 22 players suddenly remember the point of the sport. Angus is trying to get hold of his ball. Everyone else is panicking and kicking the ball anywhere in an effort to get the deciding goal. Now it's harder because it isn't just two teams against each other and the failing light, it's two teams against each other, the failing light...and Angus. You can't let him get the ball or he will be off with it. Everyone is screaming. Angus is screaming and crying and running like a headless chicken into every potential tackle.

'It's ma ba' !! Gies it!'

'One more goal!'

'My ma's gonnae kill me.'

'Two minutes'

'Nah!!'

'One minute.'

'Gies ma ba'.'

Angus is full on weeping now. His attempts to get the ball have made him dizzy and he sits now in the centre circle (if there had been one) sobbing is little heart now. Brilliant! Makes it easier. The last goal was often a highly disputed shot that went half over a jumper, but it would have to do. No time for arguments or goal line technology, not when the ball itself is staggering into the gloom, carried off by a sobbing, disorientated and fearful Angus. Game over.

I was pretty sure we were going round in circles. One scary tree in the dark looks pretty much like another. But the nervous whistling got louder and louder and even I was pretending I could do it. I was pursing my lips and thinking happy thoughts till we got through.

Dark forces can sometimes overshadow happy thoughts and we were about to see the darkest. Turns out, not all trees are the same.

We came to a railway bridge. The first landmark of any sort to tell us we were heading in the right direction. Every single coming of age film I have ever seen will have our worldly wise boys follow the train track to the next station and to safety. I think this train track was electric, so probably not the same coming of age happy ending if we had taken that route. We didn't get time to think about it, because right there on a steep bank overhanging the train line was the scariest tree in existence. Different from the rest with their imagined scary shapes. This one stood alone. It was in full dark shadow and had a rope hanging off and something tied to the end of the rope - swinging. If more drama was needed, a fast train passed, with its horn screaming, under the bridge and seemingly taking out the swinging...thing. I say 'seemingly' because we didn't stick around to find out.

I am sure to this day that despite our dream to fully posses super powers, that we never achieved that goal in life. Except I have never seen three boys run as fast as we did that night. The kind of running where your feet don't touch the ground. That would be wasting time. If you attempted that kind of running now it just wouldn't happen. Even assuming you got some speed up, you would be out of breath in about twenty yards. No one knows how far we ran that night. Given that Calderpark Zoo was only two miles away and we had walked a fair bit already, I'm guessing not as far as we thought. But far enough. We ended up in familiar territory. We had run through the fur coats, scorching them as we went, and straight out of the wardrobe...back to Narnia. I know, I know it's the other way round in the whole wardrobe Narnia thing, but go with it.

We were close to home and rather than sit down calmly and have a rational discussion about what we had seen or have a bit of a laugh about it, we decided it was better to say nothing. No one actually decided. No one spoke. Time for bed, No need for a shout. Not tonight.

Years will have to pass before this incident is brought up again. We will wait until we are in a pub, twenty years on, safe and slightly pissed, when one of us will finally pluck up the courage to be the one to say:

'Hey, do you remember that night we....'

And as we recount our hilarious theories, it will be the funniest night of our lives. A million light years from the scariest.

Nobody will mention heading on up to bed without actually being called up, or hunted down by an older sibling. That can happen if you are out of earshot for long enough and it's worse than the shout, because the sibling is pissed off at being sent out and the parents are pissed off at having to send out a search party, so you are in a no win, beat up from all sides, scenario.

That night we just went to bed. No fuss. Anyway, it was probably a school night at the end of long holiday period and we were so busy with school work for the next few weeks, we forgot all about it. So much so, that when it is brought up again, in that pub twenty years from now, we will all have to pretend to remember it, so insignificant was the whole incident. In fact it was so insignificant that I am making it all up now...or am I?

Methinks he doth protest too much.

CHAPTER 12

The lingering favourite teacher smell

I can smell her now, Miss McVitie. Even superheros have to learn and develop their skills and I learned from the best. Most go to the Himalayas to train with Tibetan monks on a gap year, we went to St Clare's RC Primary School. Most have cool karate style robes and a shaven head, our uniform was yellow and brown and our heads were not shaven, but unevenly trimmed by our mother who obviously had no access to dad's spirit level. When was brown a primary colour? I'm not saying brown wasn't a handy colour at times, but it wasn't cool.

I would love to remember warm summer school days when we would leap energetically out of bed and joyfully skip to school as the sun beat down on our unprotected heads. If we got sun, we burned. Bear in mind this is Glasgow, so if we got ever got sun, you were more than happy to burn. Jim and I almost made it a competition to see who got most burnt. This was easily measured by how much skin you could peel off each other's backs. Biggest bit wins. Like trying to peel an apple in one go without breaking the skin...only much more sick. These days we're rubbing ointments and creams all over each other. The only cream you needed then was the retrospective application of Calamine Lotion. No preventative measures were required when you could plaster a child with this chalky delight after a severe roasting. Horse bolted. Job done.

School days never started that way. School days always started in the dead of winter in darkness. One other point worth noting is that with nylon sheets at the peak of their popularity, you did not leap energetically out of them, in them or anywhere near them for fear of 50,000 volts of electricity   coarsing through your body. A well known fact now, but one we had to learn the hard way. Now I know in Medieval times, or times long ago, they didn't have heating in homes other than open fires, which we all now realise were the best things anyway, but we were at that point of discarding the open fire in favour of the highly inefficient, modern three bar electric fire. Just the one though, we're not made of money.

So, much like the Medieval child we had no heating in our freezing cold bedrooms. Ice would form on the windows, so they weren't doing much of a job. We were in bed, warm-ish, afraid of any sudden movement and being bawled at by our mother to get up for school. There was a solution. You simply had to put your uniform on before you got out of bed. Risk frostbite in one arm reaching for the uniform, slip everything under the covers, remove pajamas and put uniform on, hopefully the right way round first time. Not to worry about pants. You had them on already and those weren't getting changed until someone insisted. With practise you could even put your tie on and ties your shoelaces.

Then up, bowl of porridge and out into the darkness and cold. It was years later we discovered that the reason we remember it being so dark and cold so much, was because of an experiment by the Government to not alter the clocks for a couple of years. See if would have any effect. Well yes it did. It was bloody cold and dark up in Scotland in the mornings. They had to invent reflective strips just to keep us alive and stop us all from getting lost in the gloom as we stepped out into the unknown.

'I am just going outside and may be some time.'

'Of course you will, school doesn't finish till four.'

When Oates said that, I wonder if he got a much more sympathetic hearing.

'I am just going outside and may be some time.'

'Of course you will, it's minus fifty, you're weak, you're slowing us up and you'll be lucky to survive an hour out there in those conditions. But it's a noble thing you are doing Oates, sacrificing your life so that the rest of us will make it out of here alive. It shows great courage. You will always be remembered for this brave and selfless act. Don't worry, I will tell your wife and children you had no choice. They will understand, the whole of history will understand. Stories will be told and statues will be erected. You will always be in our thoughts and prayers. Go now, and die with dignity.'

'Oh right, I was just going for a poo, but...'

Mother was equally insistent on making sure we didn't come back till we had to. She had a checklist to make sure we were prepared.

'Do you have your schoolbag?'

'Check.'

'Books?'

'Check.'

'Tie?'

'Did it in bed. Check.'

'Did you eat your Porridge?'

'Yes, I should be good till dinner time'

'Have you got your playpiece?'

This sounds a bit weird, but it is simply what the modern child puts in his Postman Pat plastic lunch box with his sports drink container. A simple piece 'n' jam wrapped in foil, was all we needed, if not partaking of school dinners.

'No mother, we're having school dinners, remember?'

'Oh aye. Did you give your teacher the money I gave you

for those on Monday?

'Why wouldn't I? Why do you even ask? What do you think I did with it? What are you saying, mother?'

'I'm saying, did you give your teacher the money I gave you to pay for school dinners?

'Yes of course.'

'Stay on the path.'

'Oh great, now there are werewolves too.'

It may have only been a couple of years, but when you are experiencing a nuclear winter, it feels like every morning was like that. I don't remember it any other way, but I am also conscious of my natural propensity to lay it on thick for dramatic purposes. Still, I lived through it, I deserve to milk it.

Other than the nuclear winter mornings, I found primary school a bit of a breeze academically. This academic ease was not to last however, so I'm not really sure what kind of grounding it was. I was not prepared for how hard it got after that. I was at the top of my game. Peaked too early it would seem. We were tested and we didn't cry about it like now. At least I didn't. I gave no thought to those who might have been struggling. They were there to be beaten. I was top of the class. Okay not strictly true as it was always between me and John Callaghan for top spot. John was a bright lad and usually first if I'm honest. I was second top of the class, normally. Still not too bad I thought. If this is how easy life is, this whole journey is going to be a cakewalk.

I loved a spelling bee. Bring it on. Girls on one side of the room, boys facing them on the other, and the prize of a succulent, juicy orange gleaming on Miss McVitie's desk. I am having that. I don't even like oranges, but I am having that one.

'Spell...Constantinople.'

'C..O..N..S..T..A..N..T..I..N..O..P..L..E.' Nailed it.

'Consequently.'

'C..O..N..C..E..'

No! Another one bites the dust

'Outrageous.'

Easy...'O..U..T..R..A..G..E..O..U..S.' Make them harder, miss.

'Mississippi.'

Maureen Colvin's up. She's good, but she'll never get that. M..I..S..S..I..S..I..

She didn't. She's out. Schoolgirl error.

Just me and John left...again.

We bat a few easy ones around to make it a contest, then I get thrown a curve ball

'Daredevil.'

What? Is she kidding? Is she trying to tell me something? Does Miss McVitie know my secret identity and trying to out me in public? I can't show any emotion. Miss McVitie stares, waiting. For the first time I am reading more into that look. It wasn't just saying 'You're my favourite' anymore, it was saying 'Who are you really, Joseph Graham?' Is she is some kind of villain, living in a house shaped like her head, teaming up with other villains? Have they managed to control her mind to get close to me and o their dirty work. Is she a cyborg? I couldn't tell anymore.

It's an easy word, of course it is, even without a quick glance at my membership card, which I was now slipping slowly out of my pocket in case I have to brandish it and leap into action. If I make it look too easy, everyone will know my identity and I might have to kill them all to keep my secret safe. Oh no, sorry, I forgot I'm a good guy, not an evil genius, despite my genius at spelling. What do all the good superheros do in these situations?

You see this is why it is vital to make squillions and live in a cave. Living in the general population is too risky for the average superhero and their loved ones. When I say loved ones, I am not talking about my family. They can take care of themselves, besides at least one other family member is also a Daredevil, so why is it all down to me? By loved ones I am obviously talking about Ann Hay. She is sat across from me with that quizzical look Clark Kent gets from Lois Lane all the time. Ann's been sat for a while to be honest. Ann was my first love but it wasn't her brains that were the attraction.

Whoa, hold on! Not like that.

Young girls of that era did not have 'bits' before their time and did not dress like Katie Price at a gypsy wedding. Truth be told, Ann was a bit scruffy and down at heel, and this is coming from me. She came to our class as a new girl and I fell for her homely charms and cute face. She was different and had a bad, do it yourself, haircut like mine. I followed her around the playground like a puppy, and sometimes half way home. People call it stalking these days. We always have to make things sound wrong now. It wasn't wrong, and in the words of the song. 'If stalking you is wrong, I don't wanna be right.' Or something like that.

She was oblivious to all of this. I tried my best, at playtimes, to let her know how deep my love was. I kicked her a few times - playfully; punched her arm on occasion; ignored her. Nothing seemed to work. So she never knew I truly loved her. Which meant she was safe. That's the sacrifice you have to make as a Daredevil. She was as safe as the rest of the entire female population until I reached the age of seventeen. To be fair, even now, only two women have been remotely at risk of kidnap or being tied up and hung upside down over a fiery pit as I decide to save them or a bus load of school kids. I have done my bit to keep my fair share of the female population safe from evil.

I'm looking at Miss now and I can read the look in her eyes again. It is an easy read now.

'Get the fuck on with it will you, kid?'

I'm guessing it was just coincidence. I spell it nonchalantly and slip my membership card safely back into my pocket. Nothing to see. John's up.

'Accommodate'

So glad that wasn't me. I can't even spell that now. John fluffs it. It's his nemesis. I only have to spell my word and I am champion once more.

'Miscellaneous.'

It's a tricky one.

'M..I..S..C..E..L...' I throw in a slight hesitation for dramatic effect, and because I'm not sure if there are two Ls.

..L..A..N..E..

Miss McVitie isn't stopping me, I'm home free. It's the simplest of 'ous' finishes.

..O..U..S.'

Yes! Yes!! Get in. I leap onto a desk, do a back flip, pull my jumper and shirt over my head and run around the classroom with a mocking, in your face, point to all my rivals, until I realise I still have my jim-jams on under my clothes. Who cares? I win. Losers. I do the L thing with my fingers on my forehead and finally drop my trousers in a final show of...No of course I don't. You should know me by now, unless you are dipping in and out of this book non-chronologically.

C..H..R..O..N..O..L..O..G..I..C..A..L..L..Y. I can't help it, I'm on a roll.

Reality is that Miss McVitie forces everyone to clap politely. I blush. She gives me the orange. I blush even more, and we all sit down and get on with our work. I am left with an orange that I don't know what to do with. You can't eat it. It's too potentially messy. It could be dry one, but what if it's juicy? It could be a mild one, but what if makes my eyes go all funny like a grapefruit? There are too many variables and unknowns in an orange, which is why I have never really got on with them. I put it in my desk where it will live until it grows enough mould, and it's own consciousness, to leave school on its own.

The orange didn't make it home with my other prizes. Oh yes there were prizes. Books mostly. End of year test meant that top three got books with a lovely inscription from Miss McVitie. I always got a book, but for some reason only remember two. 'Around the World in Eighty Days', which followed me, if not around the world, around these isles, until I lost it a house move. Gutted. How do you lose a book that you have put in a box marked 'BOOKS' with all the other crappy books you couldn't give a shit about? I have shelves now full of old Reader's Digest books; novels that I have never read or have any intention of reading; an atlas that is so out of date some countries no longer exist and some weren't even invented yet. Which leads me to my other prize book, 'Escape from Yugoslavia'. A mighty tome of a book it seemed. No idea why you would give this to a ten year old. I tried to read it but it was unsurprisingly heavy going and I think the title might have been a spoiler. But it was my prize, so it was going nowhere. That is until Mr Campbell next door went into hospital and I agreed to let my dad take my book in for him to read. That was going to cheer him right up.

Why not though? It was a hospital. Mr Campbell was coming back out I assumed. No problem. He came back out alright, but my book didn't. I never saw it again and never felt able to bring up the subject of why he didn't think it important to return my prize book. Instead he gave it the hospital library.

Oh well, that's alright then. It's not as if it was my prize book or anything. But you know what? If the fucking hospital had a fucking library, why did he need my fucking book in the first place??

Sorry...I'm over it really.

My last memory of Mr and Mrs Campbell was when I was cajoled, because of my artistic leanings, into making them a fancy dress costume of the new 50p and 10p decimal coins, which I had to draw onto silver foil wrapped around cardboard for them to wear like A boards. This became more of a chore than a favour as all I could think about the whole time was him not giving me back my book, while I was making him look like the belle of the frickin' ball. I have never felt Cinderella's pain more.

I am sure lots of sick people still get great pleasure, if not suspense, from picking up 'Escape from Yugoslavia'- not the hernia patients - and reading the hand written inscription from Miss McVitie.

To Joseph (she called me Joseph) *for your excellent work throughout the year and for being my favourite of all time and the cutest child I have ever taught or ever will. I know I seem old to you know, but I think there may only be ten years between us, so why not look me up when you are twenty and maybe it wont be too late...PS. I know who you are DD xx*

Miss M.

Or something like that. I don't remember it verbatim, because I don't have the bloody book do I?

Footnote: What a wonderful world we live in now. Just seen the book online. I notice that it is actually called 'Escape *through* Yugoslavia', not *from*. Well that's a whole different story. If they are escaping *through*, where are they escaping *from?* More importantly where are they escaping *to?* Yugoslavia is almost incidental. I need to refer back to my old atlas. I have done its writer, Cmdr Tom Thompson, a disservice. Seems there might have been quite the complicated, suspense filled, plot after all. I also note that it is a children's book, so what was Mr Campbell doing with it anyway?

Online as a first edition, it was selling for all of £3.50. I cried a little and heaved a slight sigh that at least it wasn't an investment opportunity lost.

Juts as well really, I would have blown it if it was worth millions, or even a tenner. Never been good with money. If I get money in my hands I want to spend it, or waste it, if they aren't the same thing. Vast amounts of money didn't end up in our hands very often, but the one time it did, as expected, it only led to corruption and deceit in the great dinner money scam of '69. It has to be pointed out and fully understood, that school dinners were awful. More than awful. Inedible. I fully applaud Jamie Oliver's efforts to ban the turkey twizzler. I get it. It's rubbish and not good for our children's health. But we would have killed for a turkey twizzler...or anything that twizzled. Or anything that had a taste or looked more appealing than semolina and prunes. These days that's a health food, but it was horrible. School dinners were grey, overcooked food for adults and not designed to appeal to children. We have gone too far the other way now, I can see that and we didn't get fat then, so that was lovely. But it would have been nice to have had the opportunity.

So you understand? You are on our side? Yes? School

dinners were a bad thing. Good. Oh, and we had to pay for them. We weren't in the 'free dinners' category. There was a stigma attached to that, meaning your parents had no money and you were poor and usually smelly. But the free dinner guy was also grateful for a hot meal, so it was always a great idea to get a free dinner guy on your table. He would eat all the stuff you didn't want to eat which was critical. Because, trust me, there was a lot of stuff you didn't want to eat, but you would be forced to eat. None of this namby pamby:

'Try it and if you don't like it, you can leave it. At least you tried eh?'

No, you had to eat it or you had to sit there looking at it until you reached the age of eighteen where school teachers had no further jurisdiction over you. Not that teachers now have to work that hard.

'Try it Miss? It's pizza and chips with a side order of chicken nuggets covered in beans! What's not to like?'

Most of us developed a loathing for peas. It was always peas. The east of Glasgow (in other words exactly where we were) is nowadays ground zero for the shortest life expectancy in the world. The world!! That includes all the African countries Sir Lenny Henry flies first class to.

There are butterflies that live longer.

It all leads back to our school dinners. If they had tried a bit harder back then, we would not have had to go quite so hardcore into snorting McDonald's burgers. It genetic now. Survival.

Mother must have normally paid for dinners by online banking or by BACS or bank transfer or something, but this particular time, Jim and I were given the actual money on a Monday morning to pay for school dinners for the week. Cash in hand. A week's worth. She gave it to us. Does she not remember what happened with the whole Bambi thing? Or the football card con? Oh no, she doesn't know about that still. Anyway it was trusting of her. Why not, we are her offspring? If she can't trust us as bag men, who can she trust?

'Here, you are take this plain brown envelope to school.'

'What's in it?'

'Never you mind. Give it to your teacher.'

'Is it money?'

'None of your business.'

'How much is it?'

'It's for your school dinners?'

'Is it safe to send us out with all that money onto the mean streets? What if we get robbed?'

'Then you don't eat.'

'Do we have to have school dinners? Can't we have sandwiches?'

'No, you need a proper meal.'

A caring sentiment indeed, but then she didn't have to try not to eat them. My sandwich request, as I discovered in my first year of art school (yes I made it), was a bullet dodged. I spent my foundation year trying to find different hiding places for my mother's mainly corned beef or cheese sandwiches. By that I mean different bins. You can't keep using the same bin outside the Art School building in Blythswood Square or the tramps get wise and before you know it, they're expecting it and complaining if it's not Red Leicester on a Tuesday.

'Don't open the envelope. Just hand it over. Don't let anyone see it and don't lose it.'

Pressure indeed. Brad Pitt will know this, but if someone says don't look in the envelope, or in Brad's case, box, you are going to look in the envelope. We looked. It was an enormous amount of dosh. On average about a shilling a day for two, so we were looking at a ten bob haul here.

'Have you any idea what we can do with ten bob a week?'

'We can feed ourselves with this. We don't need school dinners.'

'We can buy proper food. Healthy options.'

'Carrot sticks; celery; cous cous; olives.'

'Or crisps and sweeties and ginger. They're food.'

'Yes they are!'

That was enough. The plan was hatched.

So when I was so insistent earlier, that I had handed over the school dinner money on Monday morning, when innocently quizzed by a caring mother, that wasn't 100% accurate, or at all accurate. We had other ideas.

We had to independently hold our nerve when our teachers asked for school dinner money. Jim was in the school annexe down the hill from the main school building where I was, so teachers couldn't consult. As long as we kept our story straight and didn't blush unnecessarily, we would be home free.

'Not this week, Miss.'

'We are going home for dinner. Mother is cooking up a lunchtime feast. She has decided that she is capable of providing us with much more nutrition for a fraction of the cost from our very own herb garden and vegetable plot.'

I over-egged it. If they had thought it through and checked our home address, they would know that there was no garden or anything resembling a garden. There was only one mysterious garden in the square that our close backed onto. The rest was wasteland. That garden was surrounded by a high hedge and we never knew who owned it. If a ball went in there, that was it. Never seen again. Who do you ask for your ball back if you never see anyone go in or out of this garden? A little oasis in a back court that was mainly used for the middens and came into its own on bonfire night when we would make a pretty good fist of attempting to burn down the whole neighbourhood. The practice of stockpiling wood for months before bonfire night was pretty common and there was lots of wood envy going on. Midnight raids on other people's woodpiles was a common crime. I still have the scar from one raid. I don't think it was that other people's scraps of wood were more flammable, it was simply a continual game of cat and mouse, that hotted up as the big day loomed, to see who ended up with the biggest bonfire on the night. If we had penises worth displaying at that age, it would have been easier and quicker to whip them out and compare.

I say 'at that age' as if times have changed.

We never compared penises. No point. Size was not the issue. It was power. If there was a score to settle or an argument to resolve it could be done by one method.

See who could pee the highest.

It stands to reason if you were looking to challenge someone in this arena, that you would come fully prepared having had plenty of water leading up to the challenge. The trick being not to reveal your planning with any pained facial expressions. There was no grey area in this challenge and height was not always an advantage over the boy who has snuck inside and filled himself with several milk bottles full of water to come out fighting like a fireman battling an inferno. There were times this was just done for fun. If, coincidentally, everyone needed to pee at the same time, it seemed a waste not to make a game out of it.

The teachers fell for it. Sorry not that, the garden story. I do go off at too much of tangent sometimes.

I can't believe I lied to Miss McVitie, but there was more at stake here. This was our chance to live the high life and we had to grasp it with both hands. She would understand later in life if we met up and had a passionate relationship once I was twenty. We would laugh about it as we lay naked beside one another in a bed that smelled exactly like Miss McVitie.

'Ha ha ha. Do you remember, Miss McVitie, when I was ten and I lied to you about the dinner money?'

'You lied to me?'

She wasn't laughing. Grown ups, eh?

'When I was ten. You were my teacher.'

'I can't believe you lied to me, Joseph.'

'I was ten!'

'I thought we had something.'

'We did! You were my teacher, Miss McVitie.'

I have just realised I still don't even know her first name. No matter, I think a few seconds of 'everything that was wrong with that short conversation' sinking in, would have ended our relationship right there.

I am sure it is stating the bleeding obvious that olives and cous cous were not part of God's overall creation, at that point. God created the world in six days, rested on the seventh when frankly, he could have got a lot more done and then rested after that. Sleep when you're dead, God. Pretty sure God just made more things up much later to make himself sound trendy.

In the Middle Eastern translation of this book, where I am sure it will be flying off the shelves, as they clamour to discover an exotic world beyond their own, we can change cous cous and olives to chips and deep fried pizza.

Not fried Mars bars or any of that nonsense. They are just a made up thing that nobody really eats, and chip shops only sell because the media bring them up all the time. We rarely got hold of an actual Mars bar. If we did, we weren't going to waste it by frying it. It should be pointed out that if Glasgow's population dies out prematurely, it will have more to do with deep fried pizzas, not bars of chocolate. Anyone outside of Glasgow finds it hard to get their head around how you even deep fry a pizza. Ask them and look at their puzzled faces. Dominos pizza have food scientists working day and night trying to figure it out to this day. They know they could double their global turnover just by offering deep fried pizza in Glasgow.

'Ze pepperoni keeps falling off.'

'What about ze olives?'

'Zay don't know what zey are, so we don't bother with zose.'

Our basic plan for a healthy alternative lunch was hightailing on the bell, to the sweetie van, stocking up with Irn Bru, crisps, Fry's Five Centres and hiding up a close till the lunch bell went again. Fry's Five Centres were a big new thing at that point. Think of it. Fry's cream but with five separate flavours. One in each section. It's alchemy! I will never forget those. You have orange, strawberry, lemon and ...erm...frog spawn and badger's breath. We knew it was wrong. We were also sure it would last forever and we would eat like Kings for the rest of our lives. Fat Kings, who only eat chocolate, crisps and sugary drinks.

But fate dealt us a cruel blow - or a fair hand depending on your viewpoint of us misappropriating dinner money for guilty pleasure. As we waited up a close for dinner time to end one fateful day, there she was...mother!! Heading to school with younger brother Paul in tow. She was on a mission. Paul's legs have never been what you might called long, but he was being dragged behind a determined mother whose demeanor suggested we had been rumbled and the jig was up. In an attempt to destroy the evidence, we stuffed all five centres into our gobs at the same time, with no time to reflect the taste sensation that even Fry's surely hadn't imagined, and set off to head mother off at the pass.

This is where being a Daredevil came into its own. We flew above mother's head from lamppost to lamppost with a dexterity that would have had Olga Korbut drooling. A few somersaults and back flips combined with some circus trapeze skills as we caught and swung each other to overtake mother and land at the school gates as if nothing was amiss.

Yes this is what I was wishing we could do as we, in fact, ran like terrified bunnies all the way around behind the houses, trying not to cry, fall or shit ourselves to land at mother's feet in a steaming pile of guilt, remorse and melted Five Centres.

'It wasn't our fault!'

'The school made us do it!'

'They didn't have enough dinners to go round and some poorer children would have starved to death if we hadn't agreed to spend the past two weeks using our dinner money to out source our dinner.'

Of course we didn't cave and admit it right away, but mother was not easily fooled. She demanded to know our movements over the previous two weeks; she shone lights in our eyes; stuck lit matches in our fingernails; tried electric shock treatment. Guantanamo Bay would have loved her.

'Where have you been? What was for dinner yesterday? Who else was there? Where is the dinner money receipt?'

'Why did she need that? For her accountant?'

'Why are you out in the streets early when everyone else is

still inside not eating their peas?'

'First sitting. We didn't eat our peas earlier.' Jim countered. Genius.

'Is it safe?'

'Is it safe?'

'Is it safe?'

She was relentless. How did she know? How did she find out? Had one of us bragged about Fry's Five Centres around Paul. Surely not. We were too careful. Paul did look smug as we were questioned at the gates, but he had just been dragged a mile to school, so that might have been exhaustion.

She could have rumbled us at any second. All it would have taken was one single lapse. One 'Great Escape' moment of dropping our guard and that would be it.

'What's your favourite Fry's Five Centre?'

'We've never had one?'

'Really?'

'Really.'

'Is that so?'

'All we ever get is ha'penny caramels, remember?'

'Yes, that's right. Shame, you would love a Fry's Five Centre.'

'I'm sure we would, mother dear. Anyway this confection you speak of does not seem possible. Do you mean like a Fry's cream but with five separate flavours? One in each section? Surely, that isn't possible?'

'It is possible. Modern technology makes it so. Men will be on the moon soon.'

'I wish I could believe it was possible, mother.'

'It is. I love them. My favourite is pineapple.'

'Oh no, you're wrong mother, orange is the...Shit!'

One way trip to the Gulag. Our version of which would be confinement to our room until dad got home and was made fully aware of the situation. At which point our arses would be the recipients of a harsh lesson learned.

Mother was not easily fooled, but she was, in the end, fooled, by the 'first sitting' explanation. Or at least persuaded there wasn't enough evidence.

We had gotten away with it...just. It was back to peas, pickled beetroot and prunes for us till the end of primary school. We could only hope that secondary school would offer more than the fear of having your head put down a toilet. Towards the end of primary school this fear, of an initiation ceremony, was instilled in us every day.

The end of primary school itself was special though. Miss McVitie was so upset at seeing us all grow up and move on, that she threw us a party. This wasn't one of those, bring a few cakes into class, make your own hats and decorations and call it a project, party. No, a real party...at her house. Pretty sure it wasn't the whole class, only the ones she liked. It is sad that this can't happen now. Sadder still that it is hard to see a day when this genuine innocence can return. It's not innocence though is it? That's a different thing. It's trust. Trust in one another and our fellow man and woman. Without this unquestioning trust we would have missed out on sitting around Miss McVitie's coffee table in a slightly Bohemian flat eating fairy cakes, sandwiches and party ring biscuits. It was joyous. Obviously I had no idea what Bohemian was then and less idea now, but I feel justified in projecting that as my memory of it now.

One of those days where the sunlight steaming in the window catches millions of specks dust in the air that you never knew were always there. Which is beautiful and atmospheric until you think about the dried skin, hair, toenails, dust mites from dusty old Bohemian throws and wall hangings and realise, that it is now...all over the fairy cakes. We sat around munching our dusty fairy cakes, telling 'remember when' tales of our fading primary school days, laughing in slow motion, hugging each other for first time without awkwardness and promising to Skype each other as soon as it was invented. Oh and the smell. The smell of my favourite teacher would fill the air and I would remember that smell forever. I can still smell her now. Every tub of L'Oreal Men Expert moisturising cream reminds me of my favourite teacher. The truth is I doubt that she actually smelled like that. Given that it's a man's moisturiser and wasn't around then, I'm pretty sure she didn't actually use that brand. She would have had her own smell, but it doesn't matter what that smell was. That's what it is now. Confident, bold and Bohemian and all I need to do is sneak into Boots, whenever I want, and open a tub and she is right there. I could actually buy some I suppose.

It's possible that it was an awkward get together where everyone felt a bit out of place because we were in our teacher's house and no one knew what to say or do. It's possible she regretted it as she now had to entertain a bunch of kids with no noticeable social skills. It's possible that in her whole career as a teacher she had much more memorable pupils or days and that our year were nothing unusual or special. It's possible she had hundreds more afternoon tea parties with kids much more erudite, confident that she still talks about to this day.

It's possible. But I don't think so.

CHAPTER 13

The actual feeling of impending doom

We were bigger boys now. Not the biggest of course, but it was getting harder to pull off being or admitting you were a Daredevil. Try using that as a defence when your head is down a toilet on the first day of secondary school at St. Leonard's.

'A what?'

'A Darblubglugdevilglug!'

'Say that again without trying to swallow a jobbie.'

'I said you better watch out, I'm a Daredevil.'

'What's that?'

I flash my identity card, which is now soggy and falling apart.

'That's a cornflakes packet.'

'I'm making new ones. There are three of us, so if you insist on this unruly and unreasonable torture, I will have to summon the other Daredevils and take you to task.'

'Go on then.'

'Right. If you will excuse me we an re-convene tomorrow, whereupon I will have had ample opportunity to discuss this at our weekly Daredevil's meeting and determined the appropriate action to take.'

'But I am going to stick your head back down the toilet again now.'

'Do you really think that's a good...blubgluggurgle?'

'Can you see the other Daredevils in there?'

'Blubbitygurgleplop!!   Okay that's it! Prepare to face

Daredevil justice. Prepare to...to...'

It would be right at that point I would realise that, as Daredevils, we never did anything. There was no Daredevil justice. No havoc we could wreak. No vengeance we could lay upon anyone. Don't get me wrong, we talked a lot about it. We discussed these possibilities at our weekly meetings, and mister toilet man would be right up there at the top of the agenda of our AGM. But we hadn't actually done anything practical as yet.

It might be too late now. We may have to grow up fast. Up until that point we thought we were grown up. Nobody really suggested we weren't. Nobody came right and said that making dens and playing soldiers and pretending we were Daredevils and lighting fires all those other things were childish. It's not how we saw it. Children don't. It's only when adults intervene to make you feel small that you realise you are still a child. The classic 'stop showing off' from your dad is enough to make any child, no matter how small, feel the size of a Borrower. You weren't showing off, you were having fun with your mates or trying to use humour to break the ice in an awkward situation.

You know you aren't allowed anywhere near the Club biscuits until auntie Doreen and uncle Vincent have finished playing cards and had their fill. It was a joke. You were pretending to take one so that so you could play the classic empty Club wrapper trick on uncle Vincent, which he would find hilarious. It was adult humour. Apparently it wasn't, it was showing off.

The older you got, the worse that put down hurt.

My days as a child prodigy at school were also numbered. With hindsight maybe Miss McVitie was too soft on us, because what the hell was primary school playing at? It was no preparation for secondary school. Suddenly we had to know lots of other stuff. Why? I'm a frickin' child genius. I know everything don't I? Isn't great spelling enough to get me through life?

Turns out it isn't. Seems there is chemistry, physics, maths, PE. Yes PE! This was not skipping about with some bean bags and hula hoops. This was boot camp. Not only was it boot camp, but there were men in those changing rooms with us. I don't mean the teacher, I mean the other boys. Boys who were happy to get naked and strut about like men. And what, pray tell me in the name of the sweet baby Jesus, is that hanging between that lad's legs?

Yes, hanging. It hung. Mine didn't hang. It didn't have to. Mine also didn't have all that hair. This was horrific. Is this what happens? If it is, when does it happen? Why has it not happened yet? I wasn't sure how long I would have to hide and not take showers, but it looked like it was going to be some time. Our first session of basic training was to be sent on a cross-country run. The only one I have ever done or ever will. What an easy gig for Mr Whatisface. Teacher don't have names now and don't smell very good. It was all 'Yes sir! No sir! Three bags full sir!' He didn't come on the run, he just set us off in one direction, appointed whoever looked the brightest to be our leader, and headed off behind the bikes sheds. He certainly wasn't off to the home economics department to bake fairy cakes for our return. A return which, as it turned out, was a trifle delayed.

Our leader might have had the academic smarts, but he was no Bear Grylls. Before too long, once we had passed Gartcosh Mental Hospital at a fair lick, we were lost. We ended up in a boggy field with a river running across it. I say river, but it was at best a small burn. We could see the school now and it would have been the quickest way to go on. But it was too wide to leap in Bear's opinion. An opinion I shared, as it happened, though I had to try my best to look brave as mister huge bollocks of course wanted to jump across. Bear was the leader and he won out, so we had to turn back. I'd seen enough films of cowboys trying to cross a raging river to know that we made the right choice. My crushing fear was not being swept away to my death, with my horse, over a waterfall, my fear was losing a shoe and getting a bit wet. I'm like a boy in a man's world now.

Turning back took us much, much longer than anticipated. We passed Gartcosh Mental Hospital much slower this time, worn out by our efforts. You didn't want to be passing Gartcosh slow or at the back of the pack. Gartcosh was viewed in the same way the spooky home of the Adam's family would be. Hang about too long and they will drag you in, never to be seen again. Men in white coats were fully justified in indiscriminately hauling random boys in sports gear into an institution, with no mental capacity tests or checks. Our views on mental health issues have moved on thank goodness. By the time we got back to school the next period was over, search parties were out with torches, police had been called, frogmen were dragging the burn and helicopters were scouring the countryside with infrared heat sensor cameras. Okay, slight exaggeration but it felt like that. We were in so much trouble and I'm guessing so was Mr whateverhisnamewas for letting us out unsupervised. We were never sent out again, but I still had to tiptoe around the PE dressing room for the next year juggling pants, socks and vest, like the dance of the seven veils, to make sure no one could ever see me naked.

I say 'the next year', I meant the next fifty years.

Exam time came and I was 12th. 12th! Oh how the mighty fell. If I had known then what future delights were in store in my educational journey, I would have taken 12th. Bit it's arm off. But at the time I could not comprehend quite how there were eleven cleverer people in the world, never mind in that class. I was gutted. This is not arrogance at my self-proclaimed brilliance, this is primary school not telling me I wasn't as good as I thought I was. Primary school giving me a false sense of my place in the world.

I came out of there naturally assuming I could be an astronaut and ended up discovering why they were sending monkeys up there instead of me.

'Welcome to NASA. So you wanna be an astronaut.'

'Well, its expected of me. I would be letting my fellow man down not to give it shot.'

'Okay dokey, so just a few tests. Shall we start with mathematics?'

'No problem. M..A..T..H..E..M..A..T..I..C..S. I can spell anything.'

'I meant actual mathematical equations and stuff like spatial awareness and chemistry so that you can perform scientific experiments in space.'

'I was actually thinking of dropping the sciences and maths and taking art. So if you need a nice model of the lunar model made from Kellogg's Corn Flake packets and tin foil, I'm your man. I have tin foil left over from Mr and Mrs Campbell's decimal coin costume.'

'Okay, lets try the practical stuff, kid. G force training. Designed to help prevent a G-induced loss of consciousness when the action of G-forces move the blood away from the brain.'

'I think I already had that with my head down the toilet.'

'Lemme ask you kid, where did you come in class this year?'

'12th'

'12th!!? I got goddamn chimpanzees doing better than 12th.'

'I am a fully trained Daredevil if that helps.'

I was not ready for this changing world. I didn't have the mental equipment or it seems, if mister huge bollocks was the new norm for an eleven or twelve year old, the physical equipment.

We were still altar boys, but it was becoming clear that we were now considered veterans. Ironic considering most altar duties are performed now by men in their sixties. We were tired, we had done several tours of duty and we wanted out. Everyone could see that we had done our bit for God and Father Rogers, so we felt sure that medals would be pinned; OBEs would be in the post; and ticker tape parades planned. All we had to do was let our dad know that we wanted out and we would be back in civvies, genuflecting in the cheap seats with the unsaved, before we knew it.

No.

Dad was not, what you might call, sympathetic to our situation. He went mental. Quitting the service of the Lord was not an option. We dropped and did twenty Hail Marys; he water boarded us with holy water and forced us on a five hour route march, or as we called it, Stations of the Cross.

He obviously thought we were showing off again and getting too big for our boots, so he frogmarched us to the gates of the Lord. The chapel itself, not the actual pearly gates. He was mad, but we hadn't pushed him that far yet. He took what we thought was the very modern step of allowing it to be our decision. If we wanted to quit, we had to walk in there and tell Father Rogers ourselves, 'mano a mano', or 'boyo a priesto'. We were hoping, in all honesty, that dad would tell him or we could write him a nice letter. Dad knew he had us by the short and curlies, if we had possessed any.

He marched us all the way to St. Clare's Church and stood us outside.

'Fine. Go tell him. Tell him you want to quit. Tell him you would rather go out and play football with Protestants, (they weren't all Protestants - he was exaggerating) than serve at the altar.'

Is he bluffing? Is he on our side? If we actually do it, will he kill us anyway? There is no way to tell, and of course no way to win. The danger is in those tiny moments where you think you might have won. Give in to those and you are dead meat!

Walk in there and encounter Father Rogers' wrath or worse, disappointment, and then come out and face the same again from dad. Brilliant. As you might guess we turned on our yeller bellied heels and sheepishly trudged home three paces behind our empowered father. Truth is, Father Rogers was probably already planning to replace us with younger models. I'm pretty sure if we had stayed much longer it would have been considered a theological foundation year. Maybe that's what dad was aspiring to.

That wasn't going to happen for one good reason. Girls. Not me of course, I have not suddenly leapt ahead in time to me being seventeen. Jim and Wullie were now showing an interest in sophisticated ladies. The hippy chick, Jackie Jensen, who lived above Wullie and the trollop, Mary Black who lived in a bordello around the corner.

There was no getting it on with these girls as far as I could see, but there was interest. Stirrings you might say. And once you start down that route your brain is no longer in control and your imagination cannot comprehend concepts like truth, justice and being a Daredevil. Try flashing your Daredevil membership card at Mary Black as she flashes a bit of knicker at you and see who wins.

Perhaps they would have been attracted by our footballing prowess if we had tried a bit of keepy-uppy for them, but girls just didn't seem as interested in the game then as they do now. It is wonderful these days how a stunning model can look at an ugly, awkward cross-eyed centre back with a broken nose and brain damage from heading too many bladders, and see past that to appreciate him for his skillful reading of the game. Oh to find a genuine woman like that who will not only discuss the offside rule and all it's varied evolutions, but will also provide a full analysis, over dinner, of whether your pressing game was effective that day. Premier League Footballers today are so lucky. It's not even as if the offside rule was that tricky in our day, or even deployed at all in most of our games. It only became an issue if someone overstepped the mark and was out and out poaching. Standing on the goalie's toes for the entirety of a ten-twenty-oner was seen as pure bad manners. He might have the goal scoring record of Messi, but he's going to be called out for his methods.

Trouble is by our footballing careers were all but over by this point, so there was no chance of bagging a knowledgeable WAG. We still played, but lack of pace and fear of injury meant we they were out of our league. The back end of our career was played out on the various pitches that had been worn and stamped into Narnia's landscape; Pitch 1: a large pitch for big ten-twenty oners; Pitch 2: a smaller, dusty one for five-eleveners; Pitch 3: our favourite, private pitch, just over the hill on an impractical slope, for just the three of us and our classic games of 'three and in'. Easy rules: one in goal, two out; first to three goals takes over in goal, and so on until you are spotted and offered a lucrative professional contract, or as lucrative as it was for footballers then until they all retired to run pubs.

The beauty of pitch 3 was location. It was en route to the train station, so we were much more visibly putting ourselves in the shop window. Every time we played there, we upped our game in the firm belief that every passing man was a potential scout for Celtic or Brazil. I'm pretty sure we thought Brazil might take us. All we had to be was good enough. And boy were we good enough on our day. The saves we made, the goals we scored. We had no idea then that Brazil had such a blinkered, insular recruitment process, where you had to actually be Brazilian.

We still played though, but with our career ambitions shelved, we played for fun. We even made our own goalposts out of chicken wire and old bits of wood. A rough hewn contraption normally, but much better than a duffle coat or anorak and as we knew we would never bulge the nets at Hampden Park, it was all the glory we could muster. As mentioned before, my return to Hampden Park was anything but glorious.

You will notice how short the girl section was. There just wasn't that much to write home about. There were no illicit underage shenanigans. We simply didn't have the balls, or 'the balls' to do much about it. If there were things going on up closes and behind middens nobody invited me. Jim and Wullie might manage a whole chapter on this, I struggled with one paragraph. But it was a sign of growing up and change. That is the point really. The fact that we even noticed them at all, is the point.

This is the downfall of man, the long tumble into temptation, the road to all ruin. As Don Henley so eloquently put it, this is the end of the innocence.

And before anyone brings up Ann Hay! That was love. True, honest, innocent love. I never saw her as a sexual object. I didn't know what a sexual object was or that I might actually have one myself.

Our final emergence from childhood to, if not quite manhood, at least realising that 'we weren't in Kansas anymore', is when the games got scary.

Scarier than dodge ball in the gable end, where you were not allowed out of the three sided gable unless someone had hit you very hard with a football. Quite hard pretending this is fun when you know at any moment a hard bladder or wet football was about to disfigure you for life, if it hit you square in the face. Oh, how I loved that game! So much so, that we three created our own version that didn't include bigger boys hammering balls at us. A safer version..for us. In this version, we set the rules by laying out breadcrumbs at the open end of the gable for sparrows and the like, whilst we sat at the top end. Now this appears to be leading to and early, cuddly edition of Springwatch, and really that is what it could and should have been, if we hadn't been sat with and assorted collection of stones. Yes, you are way ahead of me. Our version of Dodgeball was for the sparrows. Similar rules, similar cruel intentions. You would think the cows would have taught us a harsh lesson, and if we had seen Alfred Hitchcock's 'The Birds' by then we would have realised that cows were a safer target as there were less of them. We hadn't seen it. It only came out in 1963, so it would be seventeen years before it hit The Shettleston State. I can only apologise and expect no sympathy for all the games about to make my life miserable.

Scariest of all was the PE gym classes at secondary school. Not technically games but it was always called 'games' and again I could never see the fun in them.

'I want you to jump over that horse.'

'Horse?'

'Yes that one there.'

'You mean that very tall piece of piled up wood with a padded bit on top, too high to reach?'

'Yes, the horse!'

They lined us up and set us off one at a time. No training, no instruction as to how to do it. Just the experience of watching the few other suckers lined up before you. That's not teaching! Some made it look easy, some scrambled over, but my turn at this was embarrassing at best.

I ran and jumped or so I thought, without really knowing what kind of jumping was required. My kind of inept jumping left me flat against the side of the horse. Everyone laughed. I walked shamefully around it to the next embarrassment.

'I want you to climb that rope to the top.'

'How?'

'Just climb it!'

I got off the ground and held on for a bit but apparently that was not high enough. Not high enough not to be laughed at again. Maybe I missed a meeting, but assuming I somehow made it to the top of this rope, how was I supposed to get down? No instruction, no demonstration of the skill required. Where do you assume I have developed this sudden upper body strength? Was I meant to be doing body building classes at the age of eight?

'Just off to body building class, mother.'

'Did you finish your protein shake?'

'Yes, right after shooting up my steroids.'

'Work hard and don't bother coming home till you can bench press your own body weight.'

'Oh please mum, we were doing that at six.'

Is that what the other kids were doing while we were serving the altar of the Lord? If so, someone might have bloody said.

Outside at the high jump it was the same story. I have seen the Fosberry Flop in action and it looks highly effective, but I guarantee you Dick Fosberry would not have developed that technique faced with two inches of compacted, wet sand with a puddle in it.

'I want you to jump over that high-ish bar.'

'I understand what you are asking, Sir but there is no way to do that without breaking my back or my head.'

'Just jump.'

'Don't get me wrong, I realise that, from your point of view, if I manage this leap and look like a natural from the outset, you will be straight on the blower to the BOC to sign me up to their fast-track Olympic training programme, and look like the hero who discovered the next Usain Bolt (or a well know high jumper that no one knows - Oh, Dick Fosberry, of course), but the chances are, without any training or instruction beyond the, admittedly, highly descriptive word 'jump', this is a disaster waiting to happen.

'Just jump!'

The education system, and it's main practitioners, really knew how to inspire then. I jumped head first into two inches of compacted, wet sand with a puddle in it. Turns out, not only did it hurt, but I hadn't in the process, invented a new high jumping technique that would be adopted by athletes the world over. It was in fact, more the technique of someone being 'thrown' over a high bar. Not yet an Olympic sport, even if highly popular in dwarf circles.

The truth though is that many kids catapulted into these new situations seemed to either know what they were doing instinctively or must have spent their entire childhood practising for the day where it was all going to get more difficult. It made me wonder what the hell we had done with our time. How much time had we wasted wandering around fields, along hedgerows and lighting fires? It was on one of our last aimless wanderings that we encountered the game that would end all games.

We ran into some bigger boys, but it wasn't the usual scenario of stealing our stuff and making us cry. These were the same big boys we encountered before on our egg hunt, but this time they were more accepting of us. Perhaps because we had met before or because we weren't such small boys to them any more. We were entering big boy territory ourselves in all but the trouser department. This time they were excited to show off their latest find , but wouldn't tell us what it was. I think we assumed ostrich egg or dinosaur egg - something egg related as that was our only knowledge of them. Unfortunately, they had moved on from eggs.

We excitedly followed as they led us on. Wullie's excited hamster hand spider sense was tingling as they led us along the country road and then off-piste south towards Calderpark Zoo. We should have recognised the route but last time it was dark, and we were going very fast in the opposite direction and hardly admiring the scenery. As we cross the section of field, Wullie's hamster hand spider sense had turned from excitement to dread. We should have turned back. We should have pretended to be shouted in for our tea even though we were a mile or more away. But we kept going.

It was looming now. It was the tree. We were heading for the tree. The scary tree, beside the railway line, that we ran from that night. We still hadn't had any discussion about what we all thought we saw that night, so our fear of what we were about to witness was different for each of us. The bigger boys were laughing and even more excited as we looked at each other trying to second guess who was the most scared by what we were about to see. We were seeking unspoken re-assurance from whichever one of us was least bothered by the sights from that night. It wasn't forthcoming, as I seem to remember all three of us setting a new unofficial world record for the 1500 metres or mile as it was then. Re-assurance was certainly not forthcoming from me.

'It's a body. It's a hanging rotting corpse that has been there for weeks as rats nibble its toes and birds peck at its eyes. If we disturb it or go anywhere near, it's ghost will leap out and squeeze the life out of us, leaving us hanging alongside it for all eternity.'

There, I've said it. That's what I was thinking. The worst thing possible and we were heading right for it.

The field ended abruptly and the ground dropped away and there it was. The tree. And hanging from it was worse than I had ever imagined. Worse than any of us had imagined, I imagine.

It was a swing!

A long thick rope with a rough log tied onto the end of it. To be fair to my vivid imagination it looked like a body of sorts, but this was worse. A dead body was something we could justifiably scream at and run away from. We couldn't run away from a swing. It hung over a death defying drop and right over the railway line. That's how it looked. As if every swing took you right in front of a passing train. A grown up, no safety net, scary, life-threatening, swing.

'What dae ye think?'

'Nice?'

'Nice? Fuckin' nice? It's brullyint.'

The bigger boys had reached the age where swearing was

now a thing.

'Who's fuckin' furst?'

Take it as read that every second bigger boy word was a swear word, otherwise this becomes an uncomfortable read.

'Who's furst?'

Did I mention we had Egghead with us? No? Well that's because I was hoping to avoid that. Unfortunately this is where he was looking like he might come in handy.

'It's a bit high up.'

'It's no the height that'll kull ye. It's the express train fae Glesga Central.'

'It disnae go over the train line?'

'Aye it does.'

'No it disnae.'

'Bet ye it does.'

'Bet ye it disnae.'

'Aye it does.'

'No it disnae...'

This repeated for about two minutes until we had to concede that..

'Aye it does.'

Or it might. It looked like it might.

We had no choice. Backed into a corner, we did what any self-respecting superhero would do in the same circumstances. We volunteered Egghead. This would test whether he had what it took to be a Daredevil, even though what it obviously took to be a Daredevil was a great deal of cowardice and fear. He seemed to have the fear bit all sorted.

'Think of it as an initiation ceremony.'

'For what?'

'To be a Daredevil.'

'What's a Daredevil?'

Oh yeh, all this time we had forgotten to mention that we saw him as our unofficial butler, who was desperate to be accepted into the Daredevil fraternity.

'We are!'

'Daredevils!'

'All three of us.'

'Since when?'

'Since always.'

'Why am I not a Daredevil already?'

'You are...sort of.'

'Sort of?'

'You're our butler.'

'Butler!!?'

'You can have a membership card when the next packet of cornflakes runs out.'

'It's cooler than it sounds.'

'I don't want to be a Daredevil.'

'Daredevil butler, don't get above yourself.'

'I'm not doing it.'

'Egghead will do it!'

The bigger boys didn't need asking twice. Egghead was quickly perched on the log, with a leg either side and a bigger boy holding onto him. Just let go and get it over with. Why is he not letting go? Then a feeling of impending doom swept over us like a Deatheater sucking the life, colour and childhood out of us.

He was waiting for a train! The train was coming.

We didn't know whether to wet ourselves or shit ourselves. There was no way to persuade the bigger boys that this had gone too far and was a cruel game. They knew that. It was the point. Why are bigger boys games so bloody cruel? What is wrong with pretending? Does nobody just pretend anymore? What happened to the 'Come'n make it' principle? Just speculate about eventualities and pretend they're possible, even if they are not.

'Come'n make it, I leap across and grab a big boy and throw him down the slope so he tumbles his wulkies all the down, breaking his neck.'

'Come'n make it, I punch the other big boy, but he lets Egghead go cos I punch him so hard his head falls off.'

'Aye, and come'n make it, I fly and grab Egghead as he swings, just as he's about to be smashed by a train and carry him to safety just in time.'

'Come 'n make it, we tie up the big boys and hang them from the rope like the dead body we thought it was, till the Polis find them all rotten and maggoty.'

What happened to that?

The train was almost upon us and at the right point, they let Egghead swing.

He swings! He screams!! He is...nowhere near the railway line.

Egghead fell off at the bottom eventually as the swing jerked to a halt only inches from the ground. He scrambled up the bank and was off and running toward home. We got off lightly and swiftly followed him. The bigger boys were too busy pissing themselves to care.

The train passed, I am sure, with bemused commuters

giving the whole scenario barely a second glance, but for me it was a turning point. It was too real. All the pretence had gone out of playing now. Nobody was really playing anymore. I think that might have been the actual feeling of impending doom. Our childlike games were over.

Even though we never saw them as childlike, there comes a point where you are forced to think that way. Where you know the kind of games you were playing yesterday, you can't play anymore. It's almost a switch turning off and you can't turn it on again. The annoying thing for men is that they don't properly grow up till the age of thirty five, so it's a long time pretending to be grown up when all you want to do is grab a ball and pretend you're in a cup final. This is why we experienced the rise of the 'kidult'. Those lucky bastards were born to an age where they get to dress like ten year olds and play computer video games as if they are some sort of intellectual pursuit with complex rules, not meant for children. Who are they trying to fool? A game of Cowboys and Indians had far more complicated social rules and interaction than 'Call of Duty'. That's surely just shooting people within someone else's scenario set up.

In Cowboys and Indians you had to decide who was who, pick a side and costume up accordingly. If you had no actual weapons because your parents hadn't bought you any, you had to fashion them out of sticks. Then you had to decide a scenario within which these two warring sides would compete. Were we soldiers in a fort being attached by Indians? Did the Indians have a tented camp that the cowboys were going to attack? Had they captured one of us? Will we capture one of them, or is it shoot to kill? We had to figure out the whole scenario based on all the John Wayne films we had seen and our perceived viewpoint on who was the goody or the baddy. Of course, the Indian in films was always seen as the baddy, but that didn't really translate into our games, as it was fun to play an Indian.

Interesting social point as to whether we are truly influenced by films and what they want to convey, as playing an Indian was seen as more fun and more skillful. I digress.

A bow and arrow is a much more skillful weapon than a rifle, especially when it can also kill at the same range, assuming you can convince the other kid he's been hit. Once you're dead, you're dead. No coming back to life at a convenient moment, that only causes arguments. Argue your case as the weapon is dispatched into you. If it's point blank, then just die like a man. If there is any kind of distance, then you could win the argument and live to fight another day.

'Got ye! Yur died!'

'Ah umnae!'

'Y'ur!'

'Ah umnae!'

'I fired ma arrow right at ye.'

'Arrows cannae fire that far.'

'Mine did.'

'I fired the same arrow at ye last week and you said it didnae reach.'

'It didnae.'

'It's the same distance.'

'Ahm stronger than you.'

'Naw yur no.'

'Ah um!'

'Yur no.'

'Bang! Yur died.'

'Ye cannae shoot me while we're arguing aboot ma arrow.'

'Aye, I can.'

'Anyway ye missed.'

'I never miss.'

Our Arizona desert battleground, was 'the humps', two large gravelly mounds separated by a flat area in the middle and surrounded and linked on each side by several grassy mounds. Ideal for hiding and as an imagined fort. An uneven, level playing field for both sides.

This whole death argument takes place between the large mounds. It's complicated and it can involve wind direction; trajectory; bow type; arrow speed at point of impact and whether point of impact can be agreed as wounded only or certain death. It took the skills of the Oxford University debating society to settle it, unless in all that time, some others stealthily snuck around the grassy mounds and unloaded a colt 45 and a tomahawk into both parties.

'Got ye! Yur died!'

'Got ye! Yur died!'

'Fair enough. Good point well made. Urrgh.'

You can see how unchildish these games seemed. But childish they were, and it was time to stop. Time to call everyone out and go in for our tea one last time.

'The game's a bogie, the man's in the loaby. Come oot, come oot, wherever ye are.'

CHAPTER 14

I flit, I float, I fleetly flee, I fly

It was time to move. It may have been the very next day, but more likely it was months later, when our parents announced we were flitting. Moving. Outta here! The council had offered them a new house. It seemed fitting to be flitting now. That one magical summer of childhood, was coming to an end and we could start a new chapter elsewhere. Not how we saw it as the time of course. Not at all.

Flitting? To where? To what? To whit? To who?

To Milton.

We didn't know where that was. Our world was here. Our friends were here. What were our parents thinking? That's not how it works, surely? Parents now ask children if they fancy moving and if both five year olds don't agree, then the parents stay put and live in miserable cramped conditions for the rest of their days. Why couldn't our parents do that?

The modern parent even moves to be near the best schools, totally disrupting their own lives and leaving friends and family, so that little Malky can improve his Latin. To be honest, this might be exactly what our parents actually had planned, because our new school was the biggest culture shock I have ever experienced in all my days.

St Augustine's Secondary School was, for me, like public school. It had uniforms. Uniforms! It had Prefects patrolling corridors and playgrounds like SS guards, recognisable by the bits of extra striped braiding on their uniforms to denote their rank. We never had a uniform at St. Leonard's, which makes me think St. Leonard's was not bloody trying hard enough and maybe wasn't likely to be ranked 'exceptional' by Offsted, assuming anyone cared enough to check then. The new school had a swimming pool and vast playing fields with football, rugby and hockey pitches. It was like Hogwarts without the magic. It was also crammed to the rafters with geniuses. It felt as if I had been dropped into Professor X's school for gifted children without a relevant mutation. I had mutations, that others were quick to point out, but not the kind that Magneto was going out of his way to poach for his evil schemes. Turns out, not only did primary school lull me into a false sense of security, but so did the under performing St. Leonard's. My 12th placed ranking was about to become a distant dream as I spent the next few years clinging on to 29th in a class of 30. I think a small monkey with ADHD was usually 30th. The school also taught Latin. Latin? I was struggling with how everyone was speaking English.

People spoke differently here in the frozen north. No one went 'into' a room anymore, they all went 'ben' the room. What does that even mean? We had been transported right into the middle of a 'Broons Christmas Annual'. We had, in fact, moved all the way from the eastern outskirts of Glasgow to the northern outskirts of Glasgow, but it felt like we had moved to Shetland. Dumped miles from anywhere or anyone we knew, this was a strange and as it turned out, hostile, land.

The house was bigger, but it had to be. By this time, youngest brother Stephen was a growing boy and sleeping in with mum and dad was probably getting awkward. Paul was in with us, so there were three of us in one room. Jim and I still sharing the double bed - that too was going to get awkward soon - and Paul on the folding Z bed beside us. Not the best time to be sharing a room with Paul as he seemed to take the moving thing hardest, crying himself to sleep for a month over Paul Cornish, his best friend. Big sis Catherine had the other room, so it was getting a bit cramped I suppose.

Paul will argue that he took the news of a move like a man and he is perfectly entitled to make that argument, but he was only about eight. He took it bad! So did we, to be fair. Perhaps a few less tears, but it was a shock nonetheless. What about Wullie? What about this bond we had? This Daredevil brotherhood?

The sad thing about childhood phasing out so quickly, is that we never talked about being Daredevils anymore. We still knew the bond was there, but it was careering towards man hugs and fist bumps. It wont be until we are proper adults, like now I suppose, that we can talk openly about being fully paid up, Kellogg's card carrying Daredevils with the same or even more pride than when we actually were. For now there will be long periods of trying to show how unchildish we are, of being grown ups without getting to be 'Kidults' first.

We were expected to grow up, stop playing kids game, get someone pregnant before you're eighteen and get married, all whilst you're still a child inside. Expected might be the wrong way to put it, as no one really said out loud what was expected of us and, to be fair, getting someone pregnant before the age of eighteen was greatly frowned up. However once impregnated you were 'expected' to step up, and if shotguns were still allowed they would have been out in force. The thing is, although we not given these situations as targets, neither had we developed the social skills to avoid them happening. Condoms were not a discussion point, they were still a dirty word. The classic 'rhythm method' was all we Catholics had to go on and even then we had to figure that out for ourselves. What Rhythm? Country? Rock? Samba? Slade? We were all just guessing. Wrongly for the most part.

Regardless of how we all felt, and without a family meeting

that would consider our desperate losses, the move happened like a rousing chorus of 'My Old Man Said Follow the Van', and before we knew it we were in Milton.

Our time with Wullie never got to man hugs and fist bumps. Partly because men didn't hug and partly because fist bumps are stupid. You didn't even hug your mother, why would you hug another man, or a boy trying to be a man? You barely hugged a girlfriend before wedlock. You can easily get a girl pregnant without all that hugging stuff. Just put a bit of Barry White on and rhythm and hugging is the last thing on your mind.

We kept in touch with Wullie and he visited us a few times. The obvious intention was for us to remain close friends forever and be, as I said, 'man hugging it out' to this day. The last of his visits was no doubt the catalyst for losing touch, though. Despite my almost proud boast, if anyone asks, that Easterhouse was one of the roughest parts of Glasgow in the sixties, being true, we never saw it that way at the time. Not when you're busy being a child. It was our playground. Other than the normal playground threats, everything was still a low level risk, even bigger boys.

Milton was a few hundred yards from Possilpark, one of the roughest part of Glasgow in the seventies. Whether that is true or not, the point is it felt much more like it. Not at all like a playground. We were not yet fully up to speed on just how scary the world can be when you are not only not a child anymore, but not seen as a man either. What you are is a legitimate target.

On one of Wullie's sojourns from the east, we innocently visited a fun fair that had set up in Possilpark. I say innocent, we weren't drawing attention to ourselves by skipping around in lederhosen eating candy floss. Not that kind of innocent. I just mean we were trying to look cool, yet were completely unaware what a den of crime and iniquity temporary fun fairs actually are.

This wasn't our first rodeo. We had been to Saltcoats, Ardossan, Blackpool, all the big fun fair hot spots. We knew our way around a dodgem car. This was not an alien world to us, at least so we thought. We had worked the slots, as they say in Vegas, or one arm bandits as they say in Saltcoats. We had ridden all the rides that were cool enough to make us feel tough but not tough enough to make us cry. Nothing that resembled a swing. Keep your feet on the ground and make it look like a carousel is post-modern cool - whatever that means. Ride the carousel but don't look like you are enjoying the carousel, I think that is the key. Or take the practical stance that all the big scary rides were thrown up in a hurry by traveling Gypsies (is there any other kind, other than the ones who build houses and never travel?), and simply not health and safety inspected. No amount of courage is worth an H&S fine.

This fun fair felt different. Probably more of a just a 'fair' than any real intention to provide 'fun'. Set up on a piece of scrap land behind wooden hoardings, it wasn't Disneyland. We strolled and strutted as best we could in what was a calm, if borderline threatening, atmosphere. Bypassing the big rides with a wag of a finger and avoiding candy floss and ice cream, that we really wanted, because that was kid's stuff, we had just made it out past the hoardings when we were approached by... well, let's not call them bigger boys because it doesn't work or feel like that anymore. They were bigger, but size isn't the issue now. Aggression is the issue. Threat is the issue.

These thugs took a liking to Wullie's new Wrangler denim jacket and demanded it at Stanley knife point. With understandably trembling hamster hands, Wullie handed it over. I think all three of us were displaying trembling hamster hands at that moment and some trembling in other areas. There was a tiny flicker inside me a little annoyed that Jim and I had nothing worth stealing.

Wrangler or Levi denim was worth more than gold in the early seventies, which is why we had nothing worth stealing as we couldn't afford the real deal. Our brand of denim was cheap knock off stuff and we didn't even have China to make it then, so I have no idea where it was all made. China was still going through one of it's dynasties or cycling around after Chairman Mao, so they had no time to be making cheap clothing for the likes of us. Not until they realised that Communism wasn't making them enough money.

The only thing more precious than Wrangler or Levi denim was Wrangler or Levi denim badges. These were stolen from you while you still had the jeans on. You had to suffer the indignity of standing there while some yobbo rummages around your bottom, violating you by fiddling with your stitching. At least you were rarely made to give up the jeans themselves. Ah, the honour of thieves. God knows what they did with all the badges they collected. Maybe they kept them in a display case with all their Kestrel's eggs.

Denim jackets came right off, so were a much more attractive prospect. We ran off to report the incident. Or rather we shuffled away as the thugs gloated and then ran as soon as we were far enough away to out run them. There was no running off crying to your mammy anymore even if we wanted to. It wasn't going to work like it used to, if it ever did.

This was a real watershed incident, because from then on our points of contact with Wullie were all denim jacket related. These thugs set off a chain of events every bit as final as the big boys on the swing. They didn't know and were too dumb to care. Our childhood connection may well all have fizzled out soon after anyway, who knows? Or it could have carried on as we grew older and became Godfather's to each other's children and had many long boozy nights telling childhood lies and one boozy night recounting, once drunk enough, the night we saw the tree. We will never know that now.

We were left with visits to a police station to identify a thug whose identity I had no recollection of, but identified him anyway. Well, you don't want to waste police time or look like it didn't happen, so I identified the dodgiest looking thug in a line up of dodgy looking thugs and hoped Wullie and Jim remembered more than I do. They might not all have been thugs. I may well have condemned an innocent man to a life of crime, prison rape and knuckle tattoos.

'Alright Brian, my son, off to the cells with you. You been picked out of the line up, my son.'

'But I was just standing in to make up the numbers.'

'Not any more, chummy.'

'You asked me to do this as a favour.'

'Yeh, trouble is, son you've been nobbled, stitched, and fingered by a very respectable young lad, who comes from the mean streets, or one mean street mainly, of Easterhouse, made it out as a stand up citizen, only to be robbed at knife point by the likes of you.'

'But my mum brought me here on the bus and is waiting for me.'

'She can visit you in clink, son.'

'Don't you need evidence? Proof?'

'Not with such a definite identification.'

'What about the guy who actually did it?'

'Free to go, son. Taken his new denim jacket and gone. He wasn't fingered, you were. And given where you're heading for the next twenty years, will be again.'

'Twenty years for stealing a jacket?'

'Harsh but fair justice, son.'

'Alright, it's a fair cop, but this is the last time I do you any favours, dad.'

It went to court. Brian pleaded guilty so we never had to give evidence in the end. It all fizzled out, like we did.

We never saw Wullie again after that. A combination, I should think, of his mum not allowing him back to visit our patch; him being wary of coming back and maybe him finding new friends and a new grown up direction in life. He didn't need to be a Daredevil anymore. None of us did.

Being a Daredevil was of course way too childish by then, so it wasn't even a issue. Wullie didn't have to hand his membership card back in or fully pay up his subs, to make sure Daredevil accounts were up to date. There were no shares to buy out or costumes to hand back. In many ways it would have been great to have had that movie moment, outside the courthouse, where we all look at each other with tear filled eyes, knowing this is the last time we see each other, each of us determined not to crack.

'Right, that's it then.'

'That's it.'

'Yeh, that's it.'

'So, we'll see you then, Wullie.'

'Yeh, see you.'

'We'll see about doing that thing.'

'What thing?'

'You know that thing we were going to do.'

'Oh, that thing.'

'We'll arrange to do that.'

'Right.'

'Right.'

'Right.'

'What time's your bus?'

'Five minutes.'

'You better go or you'll...'

'I'd better go or I'll....What time's your bus?'

'Don't know.'

'Right.'

'Right.'

'Right.'

'I'd better go or I'll miss my bus?'

'Right. See you then.'

'See you'.

'See you, Wullie.'

There would be a long pause right then. It's raining, so that hides a lot of potential tears. As we watch Wullie walk off in the drizzle without an appropriate jacket, he would turn back and give a dismissive wave. Nobody cracked.

To be honest, Jim would have cracked. He's a crier. He is probably making this page soggy as we read. We didn't fist bump or man hug we simply drifted apart and got on with our lives and made new friends.

For Jim and I, that didn't prove to be quite as straightforward as I am hoping it was for Wullie. We now know Wullie ended up in Australia with still very strong connections to the east end of Glasgow. Yes, Facebook does have its uses after all.

Life in Milton over the next decade or so eventually became one of glam rock, girlfriends - one each, we were no Don Juans

- art school for me and working life for Jim, marriage and even children. That's the potted version which may well be for another volume, but our last childhood lesson of moving on making new friends, was an unnecessarily harsh one.

For some reason that no one has ever been able to explain, even those we later befriended, all the local lads took an instant dislike to us. It wasn't a whole new family moving into Westray Street and all the neighbours shunning them. No, it was just Jim and I. Everyone else was doing just fine and hanging around at street parties or swapping homemade cakes with the new neighbours, or whatever the real equivalent of that was. We had seemingly done something to upset the local Cosa Nostra. Disrespected someone's granny or dog; used the wrong fork; stepped on the pavement cracks, when everyone knows that's unlucky. Whatever serious crime we had committed, it obviously got everyone's back up and these things escalate like a virus around groups of hormone filled youths. Nobody tells us all this testosterone is coming, it just arrives one day and hits us and then, if our experience is anything to go by, make us want to hit other people. My testosterone was obviously held up in the post as I didn't really feel any aggressive tendencies and I was still dancing around the showers using my towel like a matador to hide my inadequacies.

Everybody wanted to beat us up or fight us. We couldn't walk out of our front door without some kids from the street looking to settle a score that nobody knew anything about. Nobody even came up with a reason at the time. There wasn't one. But who was going to admit there wasn't one? They had to keep up their bravado and even at times brought friends from neighbouring streets to join the taunting, name calling and squaring up. This went on for some time and most confrontations ended in an awkward scuffle as most fights between young boys do. That didn't make it any less scary to have to deal with on a day to day basis though. I am no Mike Tyson. I would declare myself more of a lover than a fighter, if that were more true, but in truth I was no more a lover than I was a fighter. I was just an awkward kid who didn't want to be punched. A perfectly natural reaction I would say.

Just as no one really remembers how this all started, no one has any clearer a recollection as to how it ended either. I do think it is connected to the time one particularly aggressive neighbour kid decided to up the ante and brought his tough nut cousin along to show his bravery and courage. This cousin wasn't even from Milton. He didn't even know who we were, but he thought himself tough and was obviously told we, or I at least, was easy prey. This 'gentleman' was preening and prancing like a peacock just outside our garden gate at me. I was in the garden trimming the hedge. I liked to trim the hedge, it was my thing. Still is. Anyway he wanted to fight me and, not surprisingly, I wasn't keen. This despite the fact I was brandishing a pair of garden shears and possessed expert cutting techniques taught to me, by our uncle Wullie on a Tibetan gap year, and could trim a hedge at forty yards, I still didn't think of them as a potential weapon. He obviously could see that as it didn't put him off. His verbal abuse was water off a duck's back to me. I was used to all that and a bit surprised that he didn't focus in on my ears. I was almost thinking I should point then out to him so he could aim some abuse at me that I understood.

Okay let's deal with the elephant in the room. It's in my room even if you didn't realise it was in yours. Dumbo as it happens. An actual elephant or rather the actual cartoon elephant. My ears stuck out, that was the problem. We've touched on this before. It was something that used to attract all the wrong attention as a child. I find it strange, to this day, that no one seems to comment on my ears. It may be that as we grow into adulthood that we are all too mature to mention it. Or maybe my ears just not as big and sticky outy as they were back then. I think the truth is that my head has grown into them. They were big back then and stuck out a lot. There are several ear references this chump could have went with.

When Jim and Wullie had enough of me hanging around or just felt like a bit of a laugh at my expense, all of the creative ear songs and imagery came out to play. Who knows what sets these things off? One minute you are all planning to save the world, trying to decide whether brown knitted balaclavas would work as a Daredevil costume accessory, and the next your ears are the target for ridicule. Perhaps suggesting a knitted balaclavas wasn't the best idea as nothing looked more ridiculous than wearing a knitted balaclava with your ears still sticking out. It was all we had. A tight rubber suit that holds everything in, is the popular choice for your cool superhero now and I can see why. Though I suspect you would need three butlers and a crate of talcum powder to get out of that.

Dumbo was the favourite Nom De Plume followed closely by the theme tune of the popular Nimble Bread advert of the day played endlessly on one of the only two channels. A big flying balloon to the song 'Can't let Maggie go'. Brilliant! Thanks Nimble. This catchy little number would echo around the street.

'He flies like a bird in the sky..y..y. He flies like a bird, oh me, oh my..y.'

The louder I cried at this, the funnier it would be apparently. 'Up, up and away in my beautiful balloon' was another classic that would keep the balloon and flying fun going. What is it about balloons? To this day I cannot eat a Nimble loaf. I even have a compulsion every now and again to go into Sainsbury's and smash every one of the annoying little, lighter than air, think you're so good for us, shitty little doughsuckers. Other than that, I am out of the woods.

My ears, its has to be said, were no bigger or sticky outier than Jims, but he was older and he could beat me up if I was to point that out, so I rarely made that mistake, and in those circumstances Wullie wisely went along with Jim. They, at times, obviously had important stuff they wanted to do together where I would be a liability. Like when they managed to borrow bikes from a trusting neighbour. I can see that such an occasion set them free to explore like never before. But what to do with the younger kid who is always around? He can't ride a bike and even if he had the courage to try, we only borrowed two bikes. I know! Making me run off crying was the most eloquent way to explain all that to me. There was really no other way.

'Joe, I'm sorry but me and Wullie have things we have to do and although we appreciate your input on most things, especially costume and design related topics, this just isn't a journey you can take with us.'

'How no?'

'For one thing you are as yet unable to ride a bike and this is a cycling expedition.'

'I want to come.'

'We appreciate your desires, but how is that possible when you can't keep up with the speed of a second hand racer?'

'Mum said I could come.'

'With all due respect, Joe your mother has no real say in this matter, it's all about your short legged physiology as compared to slick two wheeled engineering'

'She said I could.'

'She just wanted you out from under her feet, a bit like we do now, so you can see how problematic you are becoming all round.'

'I'm coming.'

'No you simply are not.'

'Ahum!'

'Y'urnae!'

'Ahum!'

'Ah bugggger it. He flies like a bird in the sky..y..y. He flies like a bird, oh me, oh my..y.'

Waaaaaa!!! I'm telling my mammie on...Oh that's right she doesn't care either.Waaaaaa!!!'

Off they cycled still singing. I never knew where they went on those expeditions without me. I like to think their chains broke and they felt bad about leaving me sobbing in a heap, but I suspect they were thrilling adventures and could make a whole book on their own. Not this one though.

Those are the rules of the game as a child, so you have to deal with whatever is thrown at you. When I say 'deal with it' I mean run off and cry on your own of course, not get together in group therapy and ask questions about our feelings. They do say that the two things that never stop growing are your nose and your ears. if that really is true I am in for a rough ride with the lads down the care home.

The enemy at the gate obviously saw nothing physical to latch onto or wasn't creative enough to think of any good songs about ears. He was running out of verbal abuse and building to a physical attack. He had nowhere else to go and neither did I.

However, the events of the next few seconds put an end to any more fighting or bravado on anyone's part and we lived happily ever after amongst Westray Street's 'famiglia' from that point onwards. No longer children, but happily ready to grow into men.

To be fair to the idiot thug, he had never met Jim. He had never seen Jim's aggressive side. He didn't even come from round here, but then neither did we yet. He didn't know what he was letting himself in for. Nobody did. I know Jim isn't proud of this and I am trying not to be, but at the time I could not have been prouder of having a big brother who stood up for me.

If ever there was a moment that all his Daredevil training was leading to, this was it. A superhero moment. We are not helping grannies cross the road anymore. We never did anyway. I don't recall ever seeing a granny needing that kind of assistance. Our plan were much grander anyway. We were there to protect grannies when they needed it most, ready to spring into action at any point. There just wasn't an occasion to spring into action, until now.

This is undiluted, stand up to bad guy, hero stuff. The point where the bad guy has used up all his ideas and talked all the talk about how the world is doomed. The superhero rises from the ashes and shows why he put on the suit; why he holds the membership card; and why good always triumphs over... chumps.

Jim came out of the house and in one smooth action, saw that I was being abused and threatened; saw that this kid was not one of our usual aggressors; and had obviously had enough of the shit we had taken to this point, as he leapt over the gate and landed one punch on this thug laying him out flat.

Welcome to Westray Street!

CHAPTER 15

Never go back

They say you can never go back. Not sure who says that.

You can go back. We went back a couple of times to Easterhouse, Denmilne Street and Narnia. What you can't do is go back the same way. There's a reason the wardrobe doesn't work anymore. Things move on. Time changes everything and you can't go back expecting everything to be the same.

Bizarrely enough large parts of our Narnia do look the same and are still there. No new housing development has sprung up with its own Co-op and a shiny new school. City planners came to the decision that Glasgow had gone far enough in that direction.

So all the fields and wasteland where all of our childhood happened are still there; the streets are still there; the houses still there. All looking exactly as they were but at the same time, completely different. Nothing changed, but nothing looks the same. You try to picture yourself on those spots doing the same thing, but it's hard to recognise the places even when you are right there stood on the same spot. Grass has grown over the fields and trees have been planted in an attempt I presume to make it better. Better than what? It was perfect as it was. What were mounds and hills, barely seem noticeable. The usual idea of everything seeming smaller is part of it, but not all of it.

At the time you are shaping this landscape. Your mark is on it. Those rough, half worn out football pitches were there because you made them that way by endless hours of wearing them out. The longy is that length because you kept burning it down and, without knowing you were doing it, shaped its re-growth. I think my overriding impression of the landscape when we went back last time, is that no one seems to touch it now. No one is shaping it. We struggled to pick out the different areas and their uses to us. It had all been left to let nature reclaim it. Where do the children play now? Not here that's for sure.

Going back as adults is different because you are looking with adult eyes and you can't see what we saw then. You can't look at that line of bushes and see which one will make the best den. There are moments when you revert to childhood and you think you can see those things again, but you can't. Not really. Not with the same clarity of vision. This time you are looking for it. Trying to find it. As kids we didn't have to try. We were creating it. We *were* it.

The street itself was smaller and I expected that. We all expect that. It was Narnia's main heartland that shocked me. I couldn't see it. I can see it in my head now more clearly than I could stood right in the middle of it. I suppose that is what matters most and maybe why 'they' tell you not to go back. I wanted to feel like a kid again and in truth never felt quite so grown up.

Jim and I still took time to re-enact, with our own grown-up boys, the time Paul was chased by the cows. We took them into the actual field and acted out the scenario. We had to be quick as there was also the slight trepidation that the farmer who owned the field would come out with a gun and shoot us. We always had that in the back of our minds if we ever stepped into that field and it still crossed my mind then.

Anyone watching must have wondered what the hell was going on. A bunch of burly blokes running in a field screaming like six year old girls and one angry looking bloke with horns. There were no cows that day, so one of us had to be the irate cow – sorry bull. I don't know exactly how long cows live if you leave them alone and don't try to turn them into mince. Was there a possibility that our original cows would still be hanging around with a score to settle? We would never have taken the chance, not with darker path that all cows have taken since our original encounter.

As we pointed out other ever fading landmarks and events, the boys were getting bored and it was getting harder to see them ourselves anyway. If it wasn't for the pictures still in our heads, this could have been anywhere, any patch of land and I could see that to our children that's all it was. Just another patch of land. We tried one last walk through the longy like Russell Crowe at the end of Gladiator, running our hands gently through the grass to evoke and stir the old memories, but it didn't work. Not on site anyway. It will always work in our heads and I suppose that was the same for Russell. Reality wasn't working for him either.

Our footprints are still there underneath, I know that. The marks we made will still be part of its history. The patch of land that we shaped will remain for some time now. No houses will be built there. No big developments will cover it in concrete, but for one very good reason.

Our best Daredevil den has changed somewhat. Floating Scottie dogs/grannies are now the least of its problems. What was the Monklands Canal and the border of our childhood land, is now the M8 out of Glasgow.

The best I could hope for was to point it out from the car, to my poor, bewildered wife, as we headed back south after each visit to Glasgow.

'There it is, that bit there.'

'Where?'

'There. That long grass there. You missed it.'

'There. That tree.'

'Which one?'

'Beside the railway line, look. Missed it. I'll drive next time so you can look.'

'Ready?'

'Ready.'

'There it is. Right there. Look.'

'I'm looking. What am I looking at?'

'That patch of land. We're passing it now.'

'Is that it?'

'Not just that. The tree. Look at the tree beside the railway line.'

'Oh yes, I see.'

'You don't see, do you?'

'No.'

'Bugger it, I missed the Carlisle turn off. Never mind, it means we have to come all the way around again and you will get another chance to see it.'

'Oh, great.' She sighed heavily.

The point is that it isn't special to anyone else. There's nothing to see. There are no glowing lions or centaurs roaming about. It doesn't even look special to us anymore. It looks ordinary. Just another patch of land, beside a motorway passed at over 80 miles an hour - sorry within 70 miles an hour. How many patches of ordinary land beside motorways once had this kind of life I wonder?

Batman would never have allowed this to happen. For all that Gotham City became a sprawling Metropolis, Bruce Wayne had the financial clout to make sure he never had to give up the Batcave in favour of a major motorway. Between three of us we should have had foresight to develop careers that would put us at the forefront of town planning on Glasgow's City Council, then we could have diverted that road a few yards and saved our den. Okay it would have been a bit noisy now, but even the Batcave was a bit damp and basic.

We didn't think that through at the time. We had to go and do all that growing up stuff instead. Not too much of that though if we can help it. I know that at a moments notice we could be summoned to help a granny or scrape a dog off a canal bank. Not with a Bat Signal or a Daredevil signal. Again we were remiss in not leaving a spotlighting system in place, with the local Polis, that would take us back to being Daredevils again.

We can be summoned though. We can be taken back to those moments in time at a seconds notice.

Those are the moments where you can't pass a hedge without looking for a sparrow's nest, or let a football run past you without trying some Brazilian trick to impress the small kids whose ball it is, before you overhead kick it back to them, because you never know if a scout is still watching.

You never visit a zoo because you know they're rubbish, unless you get a free pass.

You never look at an altar boy without criticising his standard of dress, or the fact he is older than the priest.

You never pass through field of cows without feeling wary and a little guilty.

You never look at a swing without that sinking feeling in the pit of your stomach.

You never crack a boiled egg too hard in case it feels pain.

You can't never resist an opportunity to light a fire and let it burn just that little bit too far.

You will never be able to moisturise without thinking of

Miss McVitie and whether you still have a shot there.

And despite how you try you find it impossible to leave a chip on a plate, because that would be a terrible waste of a potato.

The resonance is still creating ripples through our lives. Every remotely noble or kindly action or simple act of selflessness is still saving the world one tiny superhero moment at a time, even now. After all, once a Daredevil, always a Daredevil.

If I pass the right tree hanging over a river bank, I can't stop myself thinking,

'That would make a brilliant Daredevil's den. I bet no one could see me if I hid in there for a week'.

One day I might just do that.

Our piece of ordinary land shaped us and in turn we shaped it, as we grew up on it, until it was time to move on and shape other bits of ordinary land and other people in our lives.

We each took our different paths through life and whilst we weren't really looking...

...someone put a road on our cave.

END